How to Pray for Your Family and Friends

by Quin Sherrer
with
Ruthanne Garlock

VINE
BOOKS

Servant Publications
Ann Arbor, Michigan

Vine Books is an imprint of Servant Publications especially
designed to serve Evangelical Christians.

The circumstances of certain events and names of persons and
locations mentioned have been changed to protect individuals'
privacy and to maintain confidentiality.

Unless otherwise noted, all Scripture quotations in this book
are from the Holy Bible, New International Version. Copyright
1973, 1978, 1984 International Bible Society. Used by permission
of Zondervan Bible Publishers. Other versions quoted are
abbreviated as follows: TAB—The Amplified Bible, Zondervan
Publishing; NKJV—New King James Version, Thomas Nelson
Publishers.

Published by Servant Publications
P.O. Box 8617
Ann Arbor, Michigan 48107

97 98 10 9 8

Printed in the United States of America
ISBN-0-89283-670-9

Library of Congress Cataloging-in-Publication Data

Sherrer, Quinn.
  How to pray for your family and friends / by Quinn Sherrer
with Ruthanne Garlock.
    p.   cm.
  Includes bibliographical references.
  ISBN 0-89283-670-9
  1. Prayer. I. Garlock, Ruthanne. II. Title.
BV215.S445   1990
248.3'2—dc20   90-35506
                                                      CIP

Dedicated to my Heavenly Father . . .

A faithful, covenant-keeping God who keeps covenant to a thousand generations with those who love him!

To a special praying mom, my late mother . . .

Jewett Lammon Moore

And to my reliable prayer warriors, my three children . . .

Quinett
Keith
Sherry

Special thanks to Ruthanne Garlock, my loyal writing colleague, and to our understanding husbands, John Garlock and LeRoy Sherrer. Also to Servant's Ann Spangler and Beth Feia, who kept after me until this book was birthed. To all those who allowed me to share their stories, my deepest appreciation and gratitude.

To God be the glory!

Contents

A Mandate to Pray

I URGE, THEN, FIRST OF ALL, that requests, prayers, intercession and thanksgiving be made for everyone—for kings and all those in authority, that we may live peaceful and quiet lives in all godliness and holiness. This is good, and pleases God our Savior, who wants all men to be saved and to come to a knowledge of the truth. For there is one God and one mediator between God and men, the man Christ Jesus, who gave himself as a ransom for all men . . . (1 Timothy 2:1-6a)

Introduction

"SIR, HOW DID YOU COME TO THE LORD?" a young Christian asked an elderly man.

"Trouble, son. Trouble! Is there any other way?" he replied.

If things get worse—not better—in the lives of those we pray for, we can be reminded that some people don't come to the Lord until they hit rock bottom. A crisis has a way of grabbing our attention.

I know a husband whose wife prayed for him for thirteen years, and the night he had a heart attack he finally accepted Jesus. Another husband turned his life over to the Lord and quit his drinking habit when he almost died from a yellow jacket sting. A wife came to the Lord when her husband divorced her.

Our job: to remain faithful in prayer for family and friends, trusting in Jesus, the Life-changer, to intervene.

I'm finishing this book in a hotel room in Toronto just days before Christmas. This morning I pulled on my boots, buttoned up my purple wool coat and went walking in the blowing snow, just to feel it kiss my face. Being a Floridian, I rarely see snow. I loved it.

But for those not properly dressed for it, a snowstorm can be numbing—just as those for whom we pray are numbed by the enemy's assault when they are not spiritually clothed to resist the attack. And so we stand in the gap for them in prayer.

During this past year I've stood in the prayer gap with women across North America and in Germany, Belgium, Holland, and Denmark, asking God to intervene for their families and friends. Some of their faces flash through my mind as I finish this book . . .

- The mother in Germany helping to raise her teenage daughter's baby, the result of a rape.

- A Nebraska mother whose preschooler was molested.

- In Manhattan, a pastor's daughter who just had a baby out of wedlock.

- In Dallas, a father brokenhearted over one child in jail and another who is gay.

- A widow in New Jersey whose trusted close relative swindled her out of much money.

- A Canadian mother whose nine-year-old, angry over her parents' divorce, throws temper tantrums.

- A concerned wife in Chicago whose husband accepted Jesus a year ago, but won't give up smoking marijuana.

- In New York, a mom heartbroken over her son who tried to witness to and help street people, then became one of them and now lives with his pregnant girlfriend.

As distressing as each situation appears, these Christians have one common denominator: the willingness to continue praying until they see results. Many are praying for the offenders. Some are praying for God to intervene and to bring changes in their loved ones' circumstances.

They all know God has them in a place to pray—a position no one else may be willing to fill. Like the woman here in Toronto who said to me last night, "One of my husband's coworkers is dying with cancer and doesn't know the Lord. Pray for me to have boldness and the right opportunity to pray with him for his salvation and for his healing."

While many testimonies printed in this book have victory resolutions, I know there are countless praying Christians who still wait for prayer answers. Our trust must remain in our faithful covenant-keeping God with whom there is no *hopeless* situation.

This book then is for those who want to learn how to pray more specifically and effectively—for family, friends, neighbors, relatives, coworkers, strangers, enemies, and even the "sandpaper" people in their lives.

—Quinn Sherrer

ONE

A Call to Prayer

I WAS ON A NOSTALGIC JOURNEY. As I gazed across the river where a space shuttle was poised for liftoff in a few hours, many memories paraded through my mind. Here at the Kennedy Space Center area we had reared our three children while my husband LeRoy had worked as an aerospace engineer.

Walking down the main street of town, I paused at the riverbank where I used to take the kids to watch a launch. I could almost hear, "Five-four-three-two-one . . . liftoff! We have liftoff!" booming over a portable radio.

"Go, baby, go!" Quinett, Keith, Sherry, and I would shout in unison, craning our necks to see the rocket soar across the Florida sky into outer space. Clapping her tiny hands excitedly, Sherry, our three-year-old, would ask, "Is Daddy in the blockhouse? Can he come home now?"

"Yes, in a few hours he'll be home to get some sleep," I always assured her. We would sit on the hood of the car staring at the sky until the only thing visible was the tiny white contrail where the missile had slipped beyond our sight.

On that spot where hundreds of spectators used to

gather, now stood the Hickory House. As my thoughts wandered back over the years, the savory aroma of barbecue fresh from the pit pulled me back to the present and into the restaurant.

Moving toward the back of the crowded room I heard someone call, "Quin—come sit with me."

I hadn't seen Annie in years. We had become friends when our husbands worked together as engineers; our children had been playmates. But Annie's husband had been transferred out of state, then we moved to another part of Florida.

There she sat, with stooped shoulders and downcast eyes, glumly sipping coffee and smoking a cigarette. She looked ten years beyond her age.

We smiled and hugged. We'd hardly gotten past the "where are your kids living?" preliminaries, when I boldly put a question to her that startled even me.

"Annie, I don't mean to pry, but you appear troubled. How is your spiritual condition?"

"Zero," she sighed, forming a circle with her thumb and forefinger. "Just zero."

I ordered a sandwich and silently asked the Lord to help me encourage my long-ago friend.

"But what has happened to you?" she asked, snuffing out her cigarette and blowing smoke over her shoulder. "Why in the world are you so bubbly? And why are you concerned with my 'spiritual condition?' When we used to drive the kids down to the river bank to watch the rocket launches, you never talked about things like that."

"Well, Annie, my relationship with God has changed a lot since you knew me," I responded. "I've always gone to church, but now I feel that Jesus really is my best friend. Learning to pray has made a big difference in my life."

"When we moved away from here we stopped going to church," Annie confessed, aimlessly stirring her coffee. "I guess God has been with us, but I haven't prayed or given him much notice. We moved back not long ago, but we brought our problems with us. Edward and I are not getting along . . . my parents are getting older and need nursing care . . . our kids are struggling to make it. But I don't know how to help them, let alone how to pray for them. . . ." Her voice trailed off.

THE ANSWER TO ALL YOUR PROBLEMS

As she talked, I sensed this was more than just a chat with an old friend. It was a divine appointment God had arranged for me to share with Annie. Taking a deep breath and pushing my half-eaten sandwich aside, I boldly confronted Annie about her need to get back on speaking terms with God.

"He is the answer to all your problems," I said. "But you need to commit your life to Jesus and walk in his ways to receive his help. Prayer isn't just a last-ditch, desperation tactic. It's the outgrowth of accepting Jesus as Lord and nurturing your relationship with him."

Her head dropped as silence hung between us. I was asking the Lord to show me what to say next.

"Can I pray with you right now, Annie?" I asked softly. She nodded without looking up. As tears trickled down her cheeks, we prayed together. Annie asked God to forgive her for her wandering, and renewed the commitment to him she had made years earlier. The heaviness lifted, a light crept into her countenance, and a smile broke through the tears.

"All of us make the mistake of undervaluing the importance of prayer, Annie," I said, squeezing her hand. "When faced with seemingly insurmountable problems, we tend to sigh, shrug our shoulders and say, 'Well, all we can do is pray.' But actually, prayer is probably the most meaningful thing we ever do."

"I need to learn more about it, that's for sure," Annie said emphatically, "because most of my problems really look impossible to me right now. I don't even know where to begin."

The waitress refilled our coffee cups. Then for the next hour I shared with Annie some biblical principles I had found to be practical and workable in my seventeen years of learning God's ways through trial and error. I shared about praying for our three prodigal children who came back to the Lord . . . for a close relative who reconciled with his four children . . . for my brother-in-law who accepted Jesus a month before he died.

YOU DON'T HAVE TO UNDERSTAND EVERYTHING

"But does God *always* answer prayer the way you want him to?" Annie asked with a puzzled frown. "It's not that I don't believe in prayer, but the whole thing seems so mysterious."

"I know, but you don't have to understand everything about prayer before you start doing it," I responded. "Remember when some of us wives used to get threatening phone calls late at night when all the husbands in our neighborhood were working around the clock on a space launch?"

"Yes, I remember that," she replied, nodding.

"I really struggled with fear when that happened. Then my best friend Betty Anne challenged me one day. She said, 'Quin, if Jesus Christ is Lord of your life, why are you so fearful of those threats against you and your family?' "

"What did you do?"

"I was furious with my friend's question. But it made me admit I really wasn't walking close to the Lord. I knew she said it because she cared about me."

I told Annie how a few nights later Betty Anne waited outside a pastor's office praying for me, while inside I knelt and asked Jesus truly to become Lord of my life and to fill me with his Holy Spirit. He transformed my life that night and began teaching me how to pray.

"You know, Annie, prayers are something like rockets that we launch to the throne of God," I continued. "Many of my prayers have been answered and I can say, 'Mission accomplished!' Others are 'waiting prayers' I've launched that haven't yet completed their mission. But they will in God's timing. I just have to trust him and his Word. I'll be praying with you for your family, and I know you will soon begin to see that God is working on their behalf."

Annie pushed her coffee cup aside. "Well, I believe today is a new beginning for me," she said, smiling as she got up to leave.

MY PRAYER ADVENTURE

Driving back to the friend's house where I was staying, I recalled how committing my life to Jesus marked the beginning of my own "space adventure" into the spiritual realm, exploring a whole new dimension of communicating with God.

My first attempts to pray aloud were awkward. "I just can't," I complained to Laura, who'd agreed to coach me how to pray. "Just talk to God like you are talking to me right now. Practice praying aloud. Proficient pray-ers don't get that way without practice and perseverance," she coaxed. It took some getting used to—praying aloud even when alone—but in time I became less inhibited about conversing with my Heavenly Father.

I began talking to him more often, and waiting long enough in his presence for him to talk to me. I searched the Bible to learn how men and women long before me had prayed. I also listened as Christian leaders talked aloud to God, writing down their prayers so I could later study and learn from them.

Since I was surrounded by "space talk" in our rather technical community, the analogy of space exploration and my prayer adventure became obvious.

Each prayer, I learned, has a specific, defined goal, aimed for an exact target—much like a space launch does. Just as the engineers expect each launch to accomplish its mission, I needed to begin expecting specific results when I prayed.

Unlike men with finite minds who sit at instrument panels and control the vehicle's performance by turning dials and flipping switches, I could—with no technical equipment of any kind—send my prayer directly to an infinite, all-powerful, creator God! The One who made the heavens and the earth and everything in them. The One who made you and me.

Now, for me, prayer is approaching a personal loving Father, who says in effect, "Come, my beloved child, call

Me! I will answer you! Approach the throne of grace with confidence. . . . Is anything too difficult for Me?'' (See Hebrews 4:16; Jeremiah 32:27; 33:3 NKJV.)

How do we reach him? How do we start to communicate? As I discovered in my quest, there are some prerequisites, or "countdown procedures," to carry out before sending our prayers heavenward.

JESUS IS THE WAY

We must personally know his Son Jesus, who is seated at the Father's right hand as our Mediator. Let no one fool you. Jesus is the *only* way to God. He is not an *optional* entryway.

"No one comes to the Father except through me," Jesus declared. "Anyone who has seen me has seen the Father" (John 14:6, 9). Then he told his disciples, "I will do whatever you ask in my name, so that the Son may bring glory to the Father. You may ask me for anything in my name, and I will do it. If you love me, you will obey what I command" (John 14:13-15).

John, one of Jesus' closest followers, declares, ". . . If anybody does sin, we have one who speaks to the Father in our defense—Jesus Christ, the Righteous One. He is the atoning sacrifice for our sins, and . . . also for the sins of the whole world" (1 John 2:1, 2).

If you don't know Jesus as your Savior and Lord, stop now and receive him by saying this simple prayer:

Lord Jesus, I admit I am a sinner, and I repent. Please forgive me for walking in my own selfish ways, and wash me clean. I receive you as my Lord and Savior. I believe you are the Son of God who came to earth, died on the cross, and shed your blood for my sins. I believe you rose from the dead and are seated at the right hand of the Father in heaven. I want to live my life to please you, Lord. Please send your Holy Spirit to strengthen and empower me. Thank you for the free gift of salvation that will enable me to live with you forever, Amen.

LAUNCHING OUR PRAYER

I don't pretend to know all the "right" ways to approach Father God. A perfect prayer example is the one we call the Lord's Prayer which Jesus taught his disciples. Many people automatically recite it daily without giving much thought to its real significance. But when we pray this prayer with understanding it is a good beginning.

Once I'm wide awake in the mornings, I head for my "launch pad"—a well-worn gold velvet chair in my den where I curl up with my Bible, notebook, and pen. Since I'm expecting him to give me direction and wisdom, I want to be ready to jot down what he tells me.

We can "lift off" our prayers in various ways. Just as procedures for a space mission are written out in precise detail, so the Lord has given us directions in his Word. But prayer is far more spontaneous and varied than a space launch. Jesus instructed us:

When you pray, go into your room, close the door, and pray to your Father, who is unseen. Then your Father, who sees what is done in secret, will reward you.
(Matthew 6:6)

PRAYER COMPONENTS

Thanksgiving, praise, and worship are recommended ways to begin our prayer time. We enter his gates with thanksgiving and his courts with praise. We can sing for joy, shout aloud, extol him with music, bow down, kneel, clap, or lift our hands. (See the following Psalms: 100:4, 5; 95; 47:1; 63:4.) My "quiet time" with the Lord is sometimes both lively and loud as I give him thanksgiving, praise, and worship.

Before beginning intercession, it is important to repent of any known or unknown sin. The Bible says if our sins separate us from God, he will not hear us (Isaiah 59:2). So I ask God to cleanse me of my sins, making me clear and right before him as I pray for others.

Now I'm ready to intercede. Intercession—meaning "to stand between"—finds me standing between God and the one for whom I'm praying, asking God to intervene; and standing between Satan and my prayer subject, pushing back the spirits of darkness that keep him from understanding the truth.

Among the most poignant words in Scripture is God's statement, "I looked for a man among them who would build up the wall and stand before me in the gap on behalf of the land . . . but I found none" (Ezekiel 22:30). His cry was for someone to pray against the sin of the nation. His desire today is that we pray and intercede on behalf of those who are alienated from him.

PRAY FOR HARVESTERS

Though many of our family members and friends are lost without the Savior, the Bible does not specifically tell us to plead with God to save them.

We see in 2 Peter 3:9 that God doesn't want anyone to perish; he wants *everyone* to come to repentance. Jesus' whole purpose for coming to earth was to seek and save the lost, (See Luke 19:10.) and the angels in heaven rejoice when one sinner repents. (See Luke 15:10.)

Assuredly, God is not reluctant to save sinners. But Jesus did give these instructions: "The harvest is plentiful, but the workers are few. Ask the Lord of the harvest, therefore, to send out workers into his harvest field" (Luke 10:2).

Prayer is not simply asking God to save the lost, but praying that he will send out workers who will love them, share the gospel with them, and bring them into the Kingdom. And of course, we need to allow the Lord to use us to help answer someone else's prayers for a loved one needing ministry, as volunteer workers in his harvest field.

WAITING ON GOD

Waiting is a very important part of prayer. Very often we must *wait* to hear God's still, small voice within our hearts, or *wait* for him to speak to us through his Word. We would think it terribly rude if a friend came for a visit, sat down and related all his concerns, then got up and left without giving us an opportunity to speak. Sadly, many people behave that way toward God during their prayer time.

Answered prayer, I've discovered, results not from some formula, but from maintaining an intimate relationship with our Lord Jesus and Father God. Jesus said, "If you remain in me and my words remain in you, ask whatever you wish, and it will be given you" (John 15:7).

While many pray-ers spend time with God in the early morning, you may not find that to be your best time. Don't feel guilty when your pattern doesn't mirror someone else's. Biological time clocks or work and family schedules may cause us to find other practical and refreshing moments to pray. Look for the best time of day for you and stick with it.

I'm so glad I can make contact with God even faster than I can dial my husband at work. I can "fire off" a quick prayer without waiting for all the launch procedures to be in line.

In fact, I like to pray when stopped at a traffic light, or on my way into a meeting, or while waiting for someone to answer the telephone call I've placed.

STRATEGY FOR PRAYER

Prayers have different targets. The pray-er doesn't indiscriminately determine the target—it must be revealed by the Holy Spirit. But as one pastor says, *"When we aim at nothing, we hit nothing."* We should pray for the need specifically, yet leave the way that need is to be met in God's hands.

Sometimes you pray more particularly for the person concerned, or you may pray for others who influence that person, or address the enemy and do warfare on behalf of the individual.

Some days I even leave my den chair and walk the floor to pray or engage in spiritual warfare. I often pray over the world map mounted in my hallway, coming against the evil principalities and powers over various countries of the world, and praying for friends and loved ones living overseas.

Lifting off prayers to God is somewhat like shooting missiles into space, except it is far more personal, exciting, and rewarding.

Prayer

Father, reveal to me by your Holy Spirit and by your Word how to aim my prayers accurately. Thank you for the gift of prayer. Lord, please help me to hit specific targets for your divine will to be accomplished in the lives of those for whom I am praying. I trust you to give me a clear prayer strategy. Strengthen me to be faithful to the task. Thank you in Jesus' name, Amen.

TWO

Who Tells You How to Pray?

SO TOO THE (HOLY) SPIRIT comes to our aid and bears us up in our weakness; for we do not know what prayer to offer nor how to offer it worthily as we ought, but the Spirit Himself goes to meet our supplication and pleads on our behalf with unspeakable yearnings and groanings too deep for utterance. And He Who searches the hearts of men knows what is in the mind of the (Holy) Spirit—what His intent is—because the Spirit intercedes and pleads [before God] in behalf of the saints according to and in harmony with God's will.

(Romans 8:26, 27, TAB)

"Lord, I've looked everywhere for the keys and I can't find them," the eight-year-old boy prayed desperately. "Please forgive me for playing with Dad's car keys—I know I shouldn't have. But now I'm going from this spot at my friend's house straight to my room, and I'm asking you please to have those keys lying on top of the bureau when I get there. In Jesus' name, Amen."

This was a plea for help prayed years ago by John Garlock, my cowriter's husband, when he lived with his parents on a mission station in northern Ghana (West Africa). After praying he left the neighbor's house where he'd been looking for the keys and cut across the yard, following the most direct route to his bedroom. As he went he tripped on something in the tall grass. You guessed it . . . the lost keys!

God answered that earnest eight-year-old's prayer, but not according to the boy's instructions. In the process the youthful missionary learned a valuable lesson we all need to learn: God does answer prayer, but in his own way and by his own timetable.

We believers sometimes make the same mistake young John did—presuming we know how to pray for people or situations, and telling God what to do about it. But it is important that we learn to listen to God's directions for prayer, and then to follow the leading of the Holy Spirit. Thankfully, God looks on our hearts and his mercy covers our mistakes.

PRAYING IN THE SPIRIT

The verses cited at the beginning of this chapter assure us that the Holy Spirit can help us to pray according to the will of God. Jude 20 tells us, ". . . Build yourselves up in your most holy faith and pray in the Holy Spirit."

And in his famous spiritual warfare passage, Paul writes, "And pray in the Spirit on all occasions with all kinds of prayers and requests . . ." (Ephesians 6:18).

For some people, "praying in the Spirit" means to seek God's will and then pray accordingly. Others believe it means praying in unknown tongues, or in one's "prayer language." Most Scripture references to praying in the Spirit seem to imply the latter meaning.

The practice of speaking in an unknown tongue began in Jerusalem on the Day of Pentecost at a prayer meeting of one hundred twenty of Jesus' followers. They were there in obedience to Jesus' command for them to wait for the gift of the Holy Spirit to empower them to be his witnesses. (See John 7:38, 39 and Acts 1:4, 8.)

And they were all filled . . . with the Holy Spirit and began to speak in other (different, foreign) languages, as the Spirit kept giving them clear and loud expression (in each tongue in appropriate words). (Acts 2:4, TAB)

Since that time believers have found speaking in tongues to be an effective vehicle for expressing praise to the Lord as well as a powerful tool of intercession and spiritual warfare. Paul's teaching also explains the use of tongues in public worship. (See 1 Corinthians 14:18-28.)

When I first heard someone speak in tongues and sought understanding about it, a pastor explained it like this: "Praying in tongues is the communion of your spirit with God's Spirit without making use of your mind. It's praying according to the will of God, without understanding the words you are speaking. The gift is still available for believers today if you would like to receive it." (See 1 Corinthians 14:14, 15.)

I was later baptized in the Holy Spirit with the evidence of speaking in other tongues, and it forever changed my Christian experience. What a blessing to be able to pray for family members, friends, and situations with this special prayer language.

THE GIFT IS FOR YOU

If you have never received the Holy Spirit and the gift of praying in tongues, now is a good time to stop and ask the Lord to fill you. The gift was not given only for those believers who received it on the Day of Pentecost. As Peter declared in his sermon that day:

For the promise (of the Holy Spirit) is to and for you and your children, and to and for all that are far away, [even] to as many as the Lord our God invites and bids come to Himself. (Acts 2:39, TAB)

If you are a born-again believer, you are a candidate to receive the Holy Spirit and speak in tongues. You must simply ask for the gift, then yield your tongue to the Holy Spirit and allow him to pray through you. At first you may have only a few syllables to speak, like a baby just learning to talk. And like a baby's chatter, it may sound a bit strange at first, but to the Father it sounds wonderful.

Relax—go ahead and speak what the Holy Spirit is giving you to express to God. The more you exercise the gift and pray with your prayer language, the more comfortable you will feel with it and usually the more effective your prayer life will become.

THE HOLY SPIRIT, OUR TEACHER

The Holy Spirit teaches us how to pray, inspiring and directing us whether we pray in an unknown tongue or in our own language—i.e., "in the Spirit" or "with the understanding.'' Have you ever opened your mouth to pray aloud for something, then found yourself saying things you hadn't even premeditated? The Holy Spirit breathed that prayer through you in your own language.

He does the same thing when we pray in tongues, except we don't understand the words we are speaking. In some instances, however, the Holy Spirit may reveal to us the essence of what we're praying.

PRAYER RESCUE

A prayer-partner friend of mine, Mary, shared her experience of being led by the Holy Spirit to pray for a cousin she hadn't seen for several years. She and Michael had been close in childhood, but then went their separate ways and lost track of one another.

Late one night Mary awakened with this young man on her mind. She got up and went into the living room, feeling a strong urge to pray for Michael, yet she knew nothing of his circumstances. Kneeling at a chair, Mary first prayed for his protection, then prayed in tongues. After a while she went back to bed.

Shortly she awakened again, still thinking about Michael, and went into the living room to pray for him again. It happened a third time the same night, and she prayed until the sense of urgency lifted.

The next day Mary called her aunt and learned that Michael was now a pilot serving in Vietnam; she told the aunt the experience she'd had the night before. About six weeks later Mary got a report on what happened that night the Holy Spirit awakened her to pray for her cousin.

Michael's plane had been shot down by the Viet Cong forces, and he had parachuted out. His training told him to leave the crash scene immediately, but Michael crawled about fifty feet, then stopped as if paralyzed. He rolled into the middle of a bush just before a group of Viet Cong soldiers arrived, checking the area for survivors. They poked their bayonets in all the bushes around that spot—except the one where he was hiding.

When they left, Michael again began crawling away from the crash scene, but after moving only a few feet a sudden paralysis again stopped him, so he rolled into another bush. A second time, soldiers arrived, stuck bayonets in all the bushes except his, then left.

Next, Michael tried to turn on his beeper box to signal a rescue helicopter, but discovered the batteries were dead. The box could transmit no signal!

He lay in that bush for two hours—seemingly paralyzed—then heard the unmistakable whir of a helicopter coming closer and closer. It landed right next to him. "We picked up your signal!" the rescue medic said to an astonished Michael as he helped him aboard.

Did Mary's prayers reenergize the batteries in that beeper box? Or did the Holy Spirit himself transmit the signal? Who can say? The result was that three times Michael's life was spared. He was not paralyzed; his only injury was a rope burn from the parachute cord. And all three times Mary had obeyed the Holy Spirit's prompting to pray.

Had she followed what logic said, Mary might have felt one prayer that night was sufficient—after all, she needed to get some sleep! The Holy Spirit's plan superseded human logic, however, and his strategy and Mary's obedience resulted in victory.

AN URGENCY TO PRAY

Another example of Spirit-led praying was Peggy's experience. She went home for lunch one day, but when she walked in the door she suddenly felt such an urgency to pray, she did not eat.

Falling across her bed, she prayed in tongues for a while. She began weeping, though she knew of no reason to weep. Then she heard herself shouting, "I bind you, spirit of murder, in Jesus' name. You will not prevail. Spirit of murder, I render you null and void by the power and authority of Jesus Christ, my Lord."

For a long time Peggy prayed in tongues, knowing only that she was in deep intercession for something serious. She had no clue what it was. But finally she felt a release from the Holy Spirit, and she got up and went back to her work.

A few days later her older daughter called to report that Peggy's younger daughter was pregnant. She had gone to a clinic to have an abortion. But while there she changed her mind, got up, and walked out. She decided to keep her baby.

At the very time Peggy was binding the spirit of murder and praying in tongues, her daughter had been sitting in an abortion clinic hundreds of miles away. It was God's will for that baby to live, and he called on Peggy to intercede on his behalf.

I once heard a Bible teacher say, "God declares what he wants to happen, then moves on someone to pray it into existence." Peggy believes that's what happened—her prayer and spiritual warfare saved the life of her precious unborn grandchild.

PRAYER ALERT

One fall morning Billie, a praying mother in Colorado, suddenly felt compelled to pray for the safety of her son and daughter-in-law miles away in Alabama.

"As I prayed for the Lord's protection for them, it was as though I was symbolically applying the blood of Jesus to their doorposts," she reported. "I prayed first in English, then in tongues because I really didn't know what to pray about."

Later that day she learned that her son and his family were miraculously spared when a tornado hit their area, destroying much of the community. "I'm glad I didn't ignore the call to prayer," she concluded.

TRAGEDY AVERTED THROUGH PRAYER

Irene, a young praying mother in Texas, has formed the habit of praying for the schools her children attend every morning when she drives them there. On Mondays she gives extra time and attention to praying for the schools, the teachers, and the pupils.

Last year, a few weeks into the fall semester, she felt the Holy Spirit urging her to pray over the parking lot at the middle school her seventh-grader attends. She did this for three days in a row. The first two days she drove around the perimeter of the parking lot, binding the enemy from doing any evil work there, asking God to protect everyone coming and going, and praying in tongues.

On the third day Irene got out of the car and walked around the parking lot, praying and claiming the Scripture the Lord gave her: "I will give you every place where you set your foot . . ." (Joshua 1:3).

A few weeks later, a disturbed student from an abusive home shot the assistant principal in that same parking lot. The bullet missed his spine by two inches and lodged in his stomach. After surgery he recovered with no complications and returned to his job in six weeks. The student received much-needed professional counseling.

"I'm convinced the incident would have been much worse had it not been for the prayer," Irene declared. "We just never know what lies ahead when the Holy Spirit gives specific directions for prayer. We must be obedient."

SENSITIVE TO THE SPIRIT

One of the ways I've learned to be sensitive to the Holy Spirit is to pray for a person when his or her name seems unexpectedly to come to mind, or when I have a particularly vivid dream about an individual. Recently I dreamed about one of my son's childhood acquaintances who is now in the military in Europe with his young family. I awoke with an intense burden to pray that he would come to know Jesus.

Years earlier my son had shared with this friend about the Lord and we had prayed for him, but the young man responded with mockery. Now I'm following up our prayers with a letter and Christmas greeting, believing that the same Holy Spirit who prompted me to pray is working in Germany also.

A BROTHER IN THE LORD

Sometimes in praying for our own children it's difficult to be objective. We tend to be motivated by our emotions, as my friend Darlene found to be true.

Her husband died of a heart attack and her older son was killed by a highway sniper—both within one year. Sean, her only remaining child, moved back home to help her with their struggling family business.

But Darlene soon realized with dismay that Sean had strayed far from the Lord he had once served. He never read his Bible or went to church, and he was very cold in his attitude toward her.

"Stay out of my room," he barked at her one day when she had gone into his room for something. "I'll take care of my things in there."

To keep peace, Darlene tried to leave Sean to himself. But many nights she walked the floor praying for her son, pleading with God to intervene in his life. One day she went into his room to get dirty laundry and found a marijuana plant growing under a special light he'd rigged in the closet.

Standing there, getting more and more angry at the devil, she screamed at the plant, "Die in the name of Jesus! I curse you and forbid you to live in this house."

The next day the plant was dead.

That night as she again walked the floor praying for Sean, she felt the Holy Spirit leading her to pray a prayer of relinquishment: *"Lord, I give you my son. Give me back a brother in the Lord."*

From then on her prayers changed. She began to praise the Lord that Sean was going to become a brother in the Lord to her. She stopped begging God, but continued to thank him for the work he would do in Sean's life.

Two weeks later, her son came in early on a Saturday night. He knew Darlene always had a prayer meeting and Bible study going on then. Finding the Bible teacher and his wife still there, Sean began querying them. Before the night was over Sean asked for God's forgiveness and promised to follow Jesus for the rest of his life.

"God did give me a brother in the Lord," Darlene told me, rejoicing. "Almost ten years have passed, and Sean is still walking with the Lord." A prayer of relinquishment, led by the Holy Spirit, made the difference for this mother and her son.

A PRAYER OF COMFORT

Last spring, on the way to Germany with my friend, JoAnne, we sat beside a young man from the Middle East traveling with his elderly parents who were seated across the aisle. The father had just undergone lung surgery in the United States and was now returning home to live out his last days.

As the flight got underway JoAnne, a doctor's wife, nudged me and whispered, "I don't think that father is going to make it. Let's pray Jesus will make himself known to the man before he dies." During most of the night we prayed for him.

About ninety minutes before we landed in Frankfurt, the man died and his son pulled a white sheet over his father's face. Touching the young man on the arm, I said, "My friend and I are going to ask God to comfort and strengthen you."

"Thank you . . . thank you very much," he said,

dropping his head to weep silently.

While I quietly prayed in tongues, JoAnne began to sing softly a beautiful melodic song in her prayer language. A quiet calm descended not only on the son and his elderly mother, but on the other passengers nearby and on the airline attendants who were busily moving small children away from the death scene.

For almost an hour, JoAnne continued singing in her language of tongues as the Holy Spirit ministered comfort and peace to the people on that plane. We have no way of knowing all that our prayers accomplished; but we obeyed the leading of the Holy Spirit in the midst of the crisis. I believe the Holy Spirit was in charge of our seating assignment so that we could pray and intercede in that unusual circumstance.

CREATIVE WAYS TO PRAY

I've already mentioned the importance of keeping a prayer journal to note items the Holy Spirit leads you to pray about, and to record the answers. I've divided up my prayer list into seven sections. On different days of the week I pray for friends, lost relatives, missionaries, government officials, Christian leaders, etc. But every day I try to cover my immediate family, the United States president, my community, Israel, and special requests in prayer.

Above my office desk I have a large bulletin board covered with photos of many people I'm praying for.

I also keep a "traveling prayer book," a small spiral notebook with pictures of all my family members, people in our Bible study group, friends, prayer partners, and church staff members. I often leaf through this book while sitting in airports or on airplanes and pray the Scripture verses I've written underneath most of the photos. Sometimes the Holy Spirit impresses me with a certain direction for prayer.

When we ask the Lord to guide us in creative ways to pray for our family and friends we discover that his creativity is unlimited.

As we learn to pray, being led by the Spirit, God will begin to show us spiritual truths hidden behind outward circumstances. But if conditions we observe discourage us, it's important to keep our focus on the *expected results,* not on the problem! Recognizing the spiritual dynamic at work when we pray—whether in tongues or with understanding—keeps things in proper perspective.

In the natural, we easily allow our own emotions, prejudices, judgments, training, or experience to in-fluence the way we pray. Praying in tongues helps us to clear those cobwebs from our minds and focus on his intervention, knowing the Spirit always prays in accord with the Father's will.

As we ask the Holy Spirit to show us God's desire in the matter, and we yield to his direction in our prayers, God's purposes for the person or situation can be accomplished.

Prayer

Lord, I surrender myself to let the Holy Spirit pray through me for the needs of my friends and family members. Show me the things that are on your heart so I may pray more effectively. Help me to be more diligent to pray in the Spirit as you direct, knowing that I am praying according to your will. I thank you for the precious gift of the Holy Spirit. In Jesus' name, Amen.

THREE

Praying for Spouses

WIVES ... BE SUBMISSIVE TO YOUR HUSBANDS so that, if any of them do not believe the word, they may be won over without talk by the behavior of their wives, when they see the purity and reverence of your lives.... Husbands ... be considerate as you live with your wives, and treat them with respect ... (1 Peter 3:1, 2, 7)

Ford marched into the darkened nightclub at 2:00 A.M. and found his wife Janice with another man. With an aching heart he coaxed her to go back home with him.

"It was up to me, since I'd become a new Christian, to show her Jesus' love," he said. "It was a long fight, but it was worth it."

Janice smiled up at him. "I'm so glad Ford fought for our marriage," she said with enthusiasm. "God gave him eyes of faith to see me as I could be when I too accepted his Savior. I tell anyone who's praying for an unsaved mate, 'Don't *ever* give up.'"

MY TESTIMONY

"Godly submission comes from the woman who knows who she is in God through Christ—so get to know who you are in him," the seminar speaker told us.

How I wish I had heard her advice in the early days of my marriage when frankly I didn't know who I was in Christ or that he desired to live his life through me. Though LeRoy and I were active in a church, both holding offices, our walk, talk, habits, and lifestyle differed little from the lives of unbelievers in our community. But when I invited Jesus to become my Lord and fill me with the Holy Spirit, my life took on a whole new spiritual dimension. I began to share Scriptures with LeRoy, and to pray for him.

One evening, six months later, he came into the kitchen and said, "Honey, I've watched you carefully over these months and I've seen such an improvement, I want what you've got."

That night he went to an out-of-town prayer meeting, asked an elder to pray with him, and was baptized in the Holy Spirit. I rejoiced that my husband was willing to make such a strong commitment so soon after I had. Later, when our children began to stray from the Lord, we prayed together in agreement for them and God moved in the lives of all three in a relatively short period of time.

Some women pray for years and their husbands never seem to be willing to break with their worldly ties and cross over into God's kingdom. But that doesn't mean the wives are to give up praying. No, indeed. Nor should men give up praying for their wives when they seem unwilling to walk in God's ways. This chapter is for those who want to learn how to pray more effectively for their spouses, both Christian and non-Christian.

BARBARA'S LIST

While visiting my friend Barbara in Germany last spring, I listened fascinated one evening as her husband Russell, an Air Force officer, explained to a group packed into their dining room about the meaning of the Passover meal we were about to eat. As a Bible study teacher, he had spent hours preparing the lesson, the food, and the table.

After we'd eaten, I helped Barbara in the kitchen. "Russ is really turned on to the Lord!" I exclaimed. "I still remember the Sunday years ago when you asked me to pray for him. He was so wrapped up in his career he had no time for God, and he was so reserved—almost stiff in those days. But now, he is not only a mighty man of God, he's a terrific Bible teacher. What did you do besides pray a lot during the time he wasn't following the Lord?"

As Barbara shared, I jotted down her answers:

1. I had many intercessors join me in praying for him.

2. I was single-minded in my goal—determined that my words and my behavior would make him thirsty for the Lord. I asked the Lord to keep his joy bubbling out of me.

3. Russ liked to show off our home and my cooking by having company over, so I often invited Christians to share meals with us. He enjoyed that—especially

meeting Christian men, whom he found fun to be around.

4. The children and I kept going to church.

5. Russ began to go with me to a Bible study— probably out of curiosity, but also because I had such joy. Then he started going to church with the family.

Russ finally decided to make Jesus his personal Lord. He immediately had a hunger to know the Word of God, and began spending hours each week studying the Bible. Now he's teaching a Bible study group which meets in their home.

I observed Russell's tender heart toward God during my visit with them, and thanked the Lord for doing such a "good job" in answering a wife's prayers for her husband.

EXAMINE YOUR MOTIVE

I've talked with many women who believed it was their responsibility to do everything in their power to "make" their husbands become Christians. But by their manipulative scheming, they only succeeded in turning their husbands away from any interest in spiritual matters. As many wives have learned the hard way, only the Holy Spirit can reveal to an individual the truth of who Jesus is. (See John 16:8-13.)

Check your motives by asking yourself these questions: "Do I want my husband to become a Christian because I know God doesn't want anyone to perish? Or because I just think he would be easier to live with as a Christian? Or do I envision some great 'ministry' I want to embark upon, and want him to help me achieve?''

STANDING IN THE GAP

Marjorie's husband often drank too much on weekends and beat her up. Many nights he slept with a gun under his pillow. Christian friends advised her to leave him for her own safety, but she would stay away for only a short time, then go back home. She was holding on to a promise from God that her Larry would one day serve him.

For eleven years, Marjorie stood in the gap, praying, believing, and not giving in to fear—confident that God would protect her life. During this time, she was unaware that while she was watching Christian television programs, her husband would often listen from the other room. In time, the testimonies of transformed lives and his own wife's example of godliness got his attention.

Finally one day Larry went to church with her, surrendered his will to Jesus Christ, and was delivered from his alcoholism. That was five years ago. Today they serve the Lord together.

While I do not advocate wives of abusive husbands staying in a home where their lives are in danger, I'm reporting only what Marjorie did. I prayed with her during some of her most difficult years of believing for her husband's salvation. I rejoice now when I see them worshiping God together.

DITIONAL LOVE

Joan, a homemaker in Alabama, was in her late twenties and married with two children when she became a Christian.

"Accepting Jesus totally transformed my life," she told me. "In fact, my husband felt he scarcely knew this strange woman he was now living with! But to my dismay, Bradley had no interest in sharing my experience."

Joan began to pray, but nothing seemed to change. Then the Lord spoke three things to her:

1. Let me show you how to love your husband with unconditional love—just the way I love him.

2. I want you to pray that your husband will become the man of God that I, the Lord, desire to see—not the man you're wanting to see.

3. Pursue me with all your heart. Don't wait for your husband to share your interest in spiritual matters.

THE CHARACTER OF CHRIST

"With the Lord's help, I began following his instructions," Joan shared. "I stopped trying to manipulate Bradley to change his behavior. I released him completely for the Lord to work in his life. And my own life was completely fulfilled, because I was having such a wonderful time getting acquainted with Jesus."

Then one day Bradley told Joan he was going to the Gulf on a fishing trip. This had often been a source of conflict, because Joan didn't like fishing and thought he spent too much time at it.

"But this day I said, 'That's fine, Honey—have a good time!' And he could tell I was sincere . . . he was becoming the beneficiary of all God's blessings in my life, because I wasn't always nagging him about things."

Over five years' time, Joan saw the Lord make of her husband a loving, compassionate man of God—a far greater work than she could have dreamed possible. In the process she learned many valuable lessons about loving the unlovable and allowing the character of Christ to be formed in her. Today he is a godly role model for his sons and a wonderful husband to Joan.

As Barbara and Joan both learned, it's important to guard against sounding so super-spiritual that a husband feels put down. The same wise teacher who told us about godly submission also advised, "Go home and be *fun to live with!* Your husband wants a happy wife."

DON'T BOX GOD IN

We can't give God a deadline, demanding that he move by a certain date to save our mates. He does not work according to a set method or timetable. (See Isaiah 55:8, 9.)

He approaches each of us in a personal way. If there's anything we need as wives (or husbands) it is patience to wait for a spouse to join us on the believer's bench. Meanwhile, it's important to remember we are always accountable to God for our own chaste and loving behavior.

The seminar speaker I mentioned earlier concluded her talk by saying, "We women should cease from trying to be

God the Father, the Son, and the Holy Spirit in the lives of our mates. Our part is to let Christ live in us, pray for our husbands, and trust God to do the rest.''

PRAYING FOR CHRISTIAN HUSBANDS

Once your husband (or wife) becomes a Christian, you should not stop praying. In Paul's letters to the various churches he mentioned repeatedly that he was praying for the believers, and admonished them to pray for one another.

We wives must make our husbands top priority (along with our children) on our prayer lists. Our men face temptations, discouragement—even harassment—in the workaday world. They need power-packed prayer support.

WORKAHOLIC HUSBAND—FUN-LOVING WIFE

Bob, with his military training and desire to please his superiors, was a workaholic. He was driven to achieve in every area and could not tolerate inefficiency.

Annette, on the other hand, was a fun-loving redhead who was always the life of the party. She never formed lasting relationships. If problems arose, she just moved on to a new set of friends. It was no surprise that her first marriage had failed when her son was still young.

Drawn to Annette's outgoing personality, Bob proposed marriage. She married him for stability and security. But Bob, now a marine captain, tried to organize their home like a military base—complete with detailed timetable. Feeling that all the fun had gone out of her life, Annette rebelled at being treated like a marine recruit.

Bob was devastated when, after a few years of marriage, she filed for divorce. No one else in his family had ever divorced, and to him it spelled failure.

Friends tried to encourage him. "God can heal your marriage," they declared. Bob attended a Christian men's meeting and went forward for prayer for his troubled marriage. He also accepted Jesus as Lord in his life.

However, the situation with Annette grew worse. His mother said, "Bob, you're both young and you can rebuild your lives. Go ahead and give Annette the divorce. You deserve some happiness."

"Mom, what would you think if I told you I was divorcing Annette because she had cancer and could no longer make me happy?" he asked.

"I would think you're terrible!" she exclaimed.

"Well, Annette has something worse than cancer—she has cancer of the spirit," he replied. "Christ calls me to do more than seek my own happiness and personal well-being. I'm going to pray and believe God to heal her spirit and restore our marriage."

For two years Bob tried to woo Annette back. He'd say to her, "I love you," and she would scream, "I hate you!" He didn't always handle her outbursts gracefully. But he kept his faith in "the God who gives life to the dead and calls things that are not as though they were" (Romans 4:17).

Annette's hard heart finally melted as she responded to Bob's unconditional love, and their marriage was restored. She committed her life to Jesus when she at last admitted she needed him to fill the void in her life.

UNFAITHFUL SPOUSES

The Bible gives us this account of a husband with a straying wife:

> For she said, "I will go after my lovers, who give me my bread and my water." ... Therefore, behold, I will hedge up your way with thorns, and wall her in, so that she cannot find her paths. She will chase her lovers, but not overtake them; Yes, she will seek them, but not find them. (Hosea 2:5b-7a, NKJV)

God told the prophet he would put a hedge of thorns around Gomer, Hosea's unfaithful wife, so her lovers would lose interest in her. That's exactly what happened. God hedged her in, then her heart changed.

This divine hedge served two purposes: It kept Gomer from finding her lovers, and it kept them from finding her. It was a protective barrier.

Hosea's experience with Gomer can be a pattern for those with unfaithful partners. In this story we see what can happen when God puts a hedge of thorns around an unfaithful partner:

1. he or she will lose direction;

2. lovers will leave;

3. troubles can motivate a return.

A HEDGE PLUS TROUBLE

Stella's husband, Ben, had had two affairs that she knew about in their twenty years of marriage. When he moved in with the second woman, Stella reached the end of her patience.

At her pastor's urging, she and her prayer partner asked God to place a hedge about Ben so he would leave his lover and return to his family. They prayed this way for about four months.

Then Ben's and Stella's young teenage son developed a learning disorder and emotional problems which Stella reported to her husband. "That boy needs a daddy, doesn't he?" he responded. A few weeks later Ben broke off the illicit relationship and returned home to be close to his troubled son.

Did adversity prompt him to return to his wife? It seems so. Stella believes the "hedge of thorns" she asked God to put around him was the key. The whole family sought counseling. Now, seven years later, they are a restored family. Ben is still at home, faithful to a wife who willingly forgave him.

This is not a guaranteed formula for bringing back an unfaithful spouse, but it is a biblical pattern that has proved effective in many cases.

BREAK UNHOLY TIES

In God's plan for marriage, the couple's sexual union causes them to "become one flesh" (Ephesians 5:31). It literally means to be glued or cemented together—a godly bonding of husband and wife.

But concerning sexual relationships outside marriage, Paul writes:

Do you not know that he who unites himself with a prostitute is one with her in body? For it is said, "The two will become one flesh.''. . . Flee from sexual immorality. . . . He who sins sexually sins against his own body. (1 Corinthians 6:16, 18)

An unfaithful partner needs to break the unholy bond established through his or her illicit sexual relationship. This is a suggested pattern:

1. Repent for breaking God's law. Ask God's forgiveness for each liaison, mentioning in prayer the names of those with whom you had sexual relationships outside marriage.

2. Declare in the name of Jesus that all past bondings are now broken and will no longer affect you.

3. Command all unclean spirits associated with past illicit relationships to leave you in the name of Jesus. The devil has no more rights in that area of your life because it is under the blood of Jesus.

4. Thank God for his forgiveness, his cleansing, and for your marriage partner who took you back.

5. Ask the Lord to strengthen you to walk in your freedom, and "not be entangled again with a yoke of bondage" (Galatians 5:1).

PRAYERS FOR UNBELIEVING SPOUSES

I've known more than one wife who, in prayer, declared her husband to be the godly man the Father created him to be. In other words, she prayed the solution, not the problem. Here is a scriptural prayer that

has proven helpful in praying for a husband who has r.
yet seen the Light:

> God . . . grant _____ repentance leading to the
> knowledge of the truth . . . that he will come to his senses
> and escape from the trap of the devil, who has taken him
> captive to do his will. (See 2 Timothy 2:25, 26.)

Then enter into thanksgiving:

> Thank you, Lord, for the mighty man of God you want
> to make my husband. Thank you that the Holy Spirit is
> at work to draw him to Jesus, and that it is your desire
> to save him. Thank you that the harvesters are in the
> field to talk to him about Jesus. Please help me be the
> loving, kind, and helpful wife he needs, being a godly
> example for you in my own home.

A PROVERBS 31 WIFE

The same principles and scriptural prayers we've shared in praying for a husband could be applied in praying for a wife. (See additional prayers in chapter nine.)

One husband who was divorced from his wife for several years became a Christian, then he began praying for her salvation. His wife eventually accepted the Lord and they were reunited, but it took long months of persistent prayer.

After they were reconciled, he prayed she would have the attributes of the wise woman in Proverbs 31. Since some of their early marital problems had stemmed from her sloppy housekeeping, he was careful to compliment her when she cooked good meals, cleaned the house, or

ers outside their home. Gradually her self-
d confidence began to improve. Soon she was
g a younger group of women the biblical prin-
God had worked in her life.

Prayer for Wives to Pray for Husbands

Lord, may my husband be won to you without words—
simply by my behavior—as he sees the purity and
reverence of my life. God, may it be so! Lord, may my
husband treat me with respect, loving me as Christ loved
the church. As a wife, may I be of more worth than rubies
to my husband, bringing him good and not harm all the
days of our lives. Thank you for this man you've given me
for a life partner. Show me ways to express to him how
much I revere and trust him. Help me learn to pray more
effectively for him, I ask in Jesus' name, Amen.

Prayer for Husbands to Pray for Wives

Lord, help me to love my wife as Jesus loved the church.
Thank you for this special helpmate you have provided
for me. Guide me in showing her how much I love and
appreciate and cherish her. I want to be her encourager,
her covering, her refuge in time of storms. May I be a good
provider in every area of her life. Father, help us to serve
you together, I pray in Jesus' name, Amen.

Praying for a Believing Spouse

God, I ask you to fill _____ with the knowledge of
your will through all spiritual wisdom and understanding

. . . in order that he may live a life worthy of the Lord and may please you in every way: bearing fruit in every good work, growing in the knowledge of God, being strengthened with all power, according to your glorious might so that he may have great endurance and patience, and joyfully give thanks to the Father, who has qualified him to share in the inheritance of the saints in the kingdom of light. (See Colossians 1:9-12.)

I keep asking that the God of our Lord Jesus Christ, the glorious Father, may give _____ the Spirit of wisdom and revelation, so that he may know you better. (See Ephesians 1:17.)

Lord, give my husband direction for our family. Be his encourager today. May he increase in favor with you, and with his boss and working associates. May he walk in health, having his strength renewed as the eagle's.

Thank you for the plans you have for him, Lord, to give him a hope and a future. (See Jeremiah 29:11.) Thank you that you will pour out your Spirit on his offspring and your blessings on his descendants. Be the glory and the lifter of his head today.

FOUR

Praying for Children

DO NOT BE AFRAID, for I am with you; I will bring your children from the east and gather you from the west. I will say to the north, "Give them up!" and to the south, "Do not hold them back." Bring my sons from afar and my daughters from the ends of the earth. (Isaiah 43:5, 6)

I held the Valentine card in my hand and read it for the fifth time through my tears:

"Mom and Dad
If I could choose my own parents . . .
I couldn't make a *better choice* than
God made for me!
With love on Valentine's."

Underneath our daughter had added: "Thanks for bearing with us and believing in us." Beside it her only brother penned in his neat graphic artist script, "Thanks, too, for all your giving and prayers. Blessings to you. Love, Your Number One Son."

I fought the tears. They were students at the same Bible Institute out west and together they were affirming that

God made a good choice in putting them in our family.

As I thought back over their turbulent college years, right there in the post office I thanked God for being such a loving, covenant-keeping Father. There had been days when both these kids didn't really appreciate much of anything about home or us. But as LeRoy and I prayed together in agreement, the sweet Holy Spirit did woo our children back to the Lord.

I almost flew home with the precious Valentine propped up on the car dash. You may not get that excited over a note from your children, but whenever I reflect back as to how far the Lord has brought ours, I know God is a promise-keeper. As parents, our part is to live holy lives and to intercede for our children. His part is to answer!

I share many of our family's struggles and victories in my books, *How To Pray for Your Children* and *How to Forgive Your Children*, by Aglow.

GOD CARES ABOUT DETAILS

God cares about even the small details of our lives, and that includes our children's lives too. Eleanor was a Christian who knew God cared about her family, but she had a child with a very special need. Would God really intervene? After hearing me speak on prayer at a meeting in Alabama, Eleanor realized three things: she hadn't been giving God quality prayer time; she hadn't been praying with definite requests; she had never really let God speak to her through his Word.

She left that meeting with a burning desire to pray, and with a definite plan for how to do it.

Problem: Eugene, her 13-year-old adopted son, had not grown even an eighth of an inch in a year. At first she thought it was just his Asian heritage; then her doctor told her to take him to a specialist who would prescribe growth hormones.

Plan: Eleanor's habit for years had been to rise at 4:30 A.M. and run for several miles. Then she usually came home, flopped down to rest, and said about ten minutes worth of general "God-bless-us" prayers.

"I realized the time I spent with the Lord was like 'snack time,' when 'banquet time' was what I really needed," she told me. "I decided to start praying first; then if I had any time left, I'd run."

During one of her first mornings of spending quality time with God, he showed her a specific Scripture verse she could pray for her son. She paraphrased it: "Lord, may my son, like Jesus, increase in wisdom and stature and favor with God and man" (see Luke 2:52, KJV).

She never got around to taking Eugene for the hormone shots. He began to grow. In the first three months after she started praying this way, he grew three inches! In the next three months, he grew three more. Some people may argue that it was his natural growth-spurt year, but Eleanor is convinced God honored her prayer. She saw other evidence of answered prayer. Her son's conduct grade on his report card went from a C- to an A. "Mom, my teacher likes me now, and I like her," he commented when she quizzed him about it.

"Eugene increased not only in stature and favor with his teacher, but in wisdom too, as his other grades also have improved," Eleanor told me when I saw her months later.

"Sometimes he laughs and says, 'Mom, I can't get away

with anything anymore, because God always shows you when I've done something wrong.' But he's very interested to know what Scriptures I'm praying for him, and he is glad I'm praying so specifically.

"I still take time to run after my prayer time," she added, smiling. "But I find it more invigorating after coming directly from my prayer closet."

FORGIVENESS AND RELEASE

Forgiveness is one scriptural key for answered prayer. Yet many parents struggle to forgive their adult children for hurts and disappointments which accumulate over the years. Mildred, an attractive widow, shared her painful experience with me.

Her daughter Carrie, though reared in a Christian home, had married unwisely, borne a son, divorced, then gotten into drugs and spent time in jail. Mildred was taking care of the little boy, but financial problems forced Carrie to live with her. The conflict between them was endless.

"I was constantly nagging Carrie about her lifestyle, her selfishness, her neglect of her son," Mildred said. "I would leave things lying around the house for her to read. But she was hostile toward me, and our relationship just deteriorated."

A turning point came when Mildred read Dr. James Dobson's book *Love Must Be Tough*.

"I realized I had to forgive Carrie for everything she had done, and just release her into God's hands. Hard as it was, I did it. I stopped nagging and berating her, and began just to love her and pray for her."

I HAVE A DAUGHTER FOR THE FIRST TIME

The results were swift and dramatic. Two weeks after Mildred's decision to forgive and release her daughter, Carrie stayed up late one night to watch TV alone. She tuned in to a Christian program and had a "Damascus Road" experience, recommitting her life to the Lord.

"When I saw her the next morning she was like a different person," Mildred reported. "She did a complete about-face and began to serve the Lord."

After her conversion, Carrie found out she was pregnant with twins. Had she known it sooner she might have had an abortion, but she determined to keep the babies and began praying for them months before they were born.

"If I were to list all the qualities I would want in a daughter, it would be a list of all the things Carrie is," Mildred shared. "I feel as if I have a daughter for the first time—and she can hardly believe she did all those things that are in her past. She is rearing all her children in the Lord, and we have a happy, godly home."

PRAYING SCRIPTURES

When I have no inkling how to pray for a child in a tight place, God often points me to a Bible passage suitable for his or her situation. Then I pray it aloud. God promises, ". . . I am watching to see that my word is fulfilled" (Jeremiah 1:12).

When our children were in college I prayed that they, like Solomon, would have "wisdom and very great insight, and a breadth of understanding as measureless as the sand on the seashore" (1 Kings 4:29).

When my son was working as a graphic artist I prayed: "Lord, fill him with the Spirit of God, with skill, ability, and knowledge in all kinds of crafts—to make artistic designs." (See Exodus 35:31, 32.)

Later when he was in Bible School, I prayed that Keith would show "aptitude for every kind of learning, be well informed, quick to understand, and qualified to serve in the king's palace," and that he might speak God's Word "with great boldness, and stretch out his hand to heal and perform miraculous signs and wonders through the name of God's holy servant Jesus." (See Daniel 1:4; Acts 4:29, 30.)

For Quinett, an interior designer who also makes worship banners for church and home use, I've prayed for years that she may be filled "with skill to do all kinds of work as a craftsman, designer, embroiderer in blue, purple, and scarlet yarn and fine linen . . . a master craftsman and designer." (See Exodus 35:35.)

God will give Scriptures for all our children if only we take the time to ask him. As each new year begins, I ask the Lord to direct me to the Scriptures he wants me to pray for my children in the coming year. I then write them in my prayer journal in January and refer to them throughout the year.

While Quinett lived for almost a year in Israel, the land of the Psalmist David, the Lord directed me to pray many verses from the Psalms for her.

When our younger daughter Sherry and her husband moved to his native country, Denmark, I prayed a lot differently for them than I had when they were just 800 miles away attending Bible school. Psalm 91 became a prayer of protection as I often read it aloud and inserted their names.

Carleen, a praying mother I've known for some years, shared some Scripture verses she personalizes as she prays for both her sons:

I do not ask that you take Jason and Joel and our future daughters-in-law out of this world, but that you protect them from the evil one. Sanctify them by the truth; your word is truth. (See John 17:15-17.)

Lord, teach Jason and Joel how to cleanse their ways by taking heed and keeping watch on themselves according to your Word, conforming their lives to it. May they seek you with all their hearts, inquiring of you and yearning for you. Let them not wander or step aside (either in ignorance or willfully) from your commandments. (See Psalm 119:9-11 TAB.)

I pray our sons will find godly wives and together they will love the Lord with all their hearts, all their souls, with all their strength, and with all their minds, and love their neighbors as themselves. (See Luke 10:27.)

May they walk in the fruit of the Spirit: love, joy, peace, patience, kindness, goodness, faithfulness, gentleness and self-control. (See Galatians 5:22, 23.)

Carleen also personalizes Ephesians 3:14, 15 for their entire family, and Isaiah 54:13 for her children.

LEARNING TO APPLY GOD'S WORD

Jo is another mother who learned to apply the Word of God in praying for her child, but she also taught her son, William, how to use the Word for himself.

Weighed down with a poor self-image and near-failing grades, William gladly consented to the Bible recitation his mother asked him to repeat daily before he went to school.

"Who are you?" she would ask.

"I'm an overcomer; I'm a winner," William would reply.

"What's your word?"

"Greater is Jesus in me than the devil in the world."

"And?"

"I'm filled with the Holy Spirit."

"And?"

"I can do all things through Christ who strengthens me. For God has not given me a spirit of fear, but of power and of love and a sound mind."

"And?"

"I have the mind of Jesus Christ. If God is for me, who can be against me?"

They continued this practice over several years, and Jo looked for every opportunity to encourage and reaffirm her son. When William was twelve, finishing the seventh grade, he brought home a coveted honor roll certificate. He had learned to believe and to declare who he was in Christ, and his mind was indeed renewed. Across the top of the award the teacher had written, "William—You Are A Winner!"

A SON'S HEALING

As these stories illustrate, Christian parents are concerned about praying for their children's salvation, but also a host of other things—their education, friendships, mates, employment, protection, and healing. Jesus' sacrificial death to redeem us from sin also includes a provision for healing, and Scripture instructs us to pray for it. (See 1 Peter 2:24; James 5:14, 15.)

Sylvia's son, Marcus, was sixteen when he was diagnosed with terminal colon cancer, which had already destroyed three inches of his large intestine. Unable to eat solid food, he was rapidly losing weight.

But Sylvia knew how to pray and do spiritual warfare, and she called for prayer support in this crisis. She took Marcus to a prayer meeting where members joined together in spiritual warfare on his behalf and asked the Lord to heal him.

"When they laid hands on me and prayed for my healing, I felt a warmth shoot through my abdomen," he told me. "I know the power of God was in that meeting, and I told everyone I was sure I was healed."

Sylvia prepared a regular meal for him, and Marcus ate solid food for the first time in more than a year, with no ill effects. Two weeks later x-rays showed he had a completely restored intestine. He has been free of cancer for thirteen years, and is now attending Bible school.

Of course this is not an assured solution for healing, as healing can come in many different ways in response to prayer. But the fact remains, Jesus still heals people today—both physically and emotionally. He also wants to heal broken relationships.

PRAYER OVERRULES DISAPPOINTMENT

Myrna and her daughter Heidi had always been unusually close because Heidi was an only child. After Myrna's husband deserted them when Heidi was five, they moved to Asia where Myrna served as a missions teacher. The two of them lived outside the United States until Heidi reached college age.

They returned to the States and the daughter enrolled in college. But after two years Heidi came home from school one weekend and announced, "Mom, Chuck and I got married last week."

Myrna was stunned. "How could you do this to me?" she screamed. "Chuck's never been to college . . . he's younger than you are . . . he's been a Christian for only a year!"

She cried and prayed for a long time, but finally released to the Lord her desires and expectations for Heidi. "God, your Word says you will not give us a stone for bread," she declared. "I've prayed for years for a godly husband for my daughter, and I now choose to believe for your best."

Heidi soon got pregnant and dropped out of college. They moved to a small town and Chuck worked at various menial jobs to support them.

While visiting them with her closest friend one day, Myrna and Lou began rehearsing all of Chuck's faults—his foolish spending, his criticism of Heidi, his immaturity. But Lou immediately began to feel convicted about their conversation. "Myrna, I think we need to repent," she said. "I'm sorry I've participated in tearing down Chuck's character. We need to thank the Lord for his good qualities."

Myrna agreed, and they both asked for the Lord's forgiveness, then began praying, "Lord, thank you that Chuck is quick to forgive . . . he helps with the baby at night . . . he's generous . . . he does love Heidi." Over the next few weeks Myrna continued thanking the Lord for Chuck's qualities.

"By the time I went for my next visit to spend a few days with them, Chuck had stopped doing all the things I'd criticized him for after the previous visit," she said. "It was an amazing change in the way I looked at my son-in-law."

Today Heidi, Chuck, and their four children live with Myrna, and it's a happy household. "He is all the things I prayed for years that Heidi would have in a husband," she reports. "He's the spiritual head of his family, and he's teaching his children the ways of the Lord."

A MOTHER'S LETTER OF VICTORY

Recently I received a letter from Suzanne, a praying mother on the west coast which should encourage parents of wayward children. She gave me permission to share it:

When you gave a seminar in our area two years ago, I poured my mother's heart out to you, and you responded by praying for me and my son. When you autographed a copy of your book you wrote: *"Keep standing in the gap for Steven—a mighty man of valor!"* At the time he was anything but that, but I was praying for him to be mighty for the Lord.

Our only child, adopted fifteen-year-old Steven, was in total rebellion. He was deeply involved in pornography, drugs, alcohol, the occult, Hell's Angels, the

Ku Klux Klan, and organized crime. He had already robbed at least thirty homes, and had stolen numerous cars. He had also become fascinated with death.

God saved Steven the day of his sentencing hearing— the day of his greatest rebellion. He had received three and a half times the sentence he expected. In prison Steven attended Bible studies, and even though it was extremely difficult, took a stand for the Lord right where he was. After his release he worked at a Christian camp for the summer and received the baptism in the Holy Spirit. He has been attending high school at a Christian ministry . . . and plans to attend Bible college.

We knew as we surrendered Steven to the Lord before he was arrested that he would never live at home again. But we stood on Isaiah 54:13 and have seen its fulfillment. Steven is being taught by the Lord and great is his peace. When you tell women to offer their children to the Lord like Hannah did, tell them also that they may have to do so literally, but that God will also give them great peace, and more children.

I have been able to tell Steven's story to numerous individuals and have collected many children to pray for. Recently I talked to a lady sitting next to me on the airplane who also had a teenage adopted son named Steven. He had gotten into the same troubles as our son, but has not yet come to know Jesus. I was able to pray with her, and now we are standing together for her son.

My husband and I learned to pray together, to give our son to God, to forgive him, and to love him through it all. Now, our times with our Steven are precious. Yes, God is faithful; he does perform his Word!

Prayer

Father, please give me your wisdom to know how to pray for my children. I lift their specific needs to you now: *(name them)*. I forgive _____ for hurting me and disappointing me; please help me to love them with your love and to walk in constant forgiveness.

Lord, show me appropriate Scriptures to pray for them. I release _____ into your hands, and ask you to work in their lives according to your plan and purpose. I commit them into your care and trust you to draw them to yourself by the power of the Holy Spirit. Thank you in Jesus' name for your work of grace in their lives, Amen.

PROMISE FROM GOD FOR CHILDREN OF BELIEVERS

"As for me, this is my covenant with them," says the LORD. "My Spirit, who is on you, and my words that I have put in your mouth will not depart from your mouth, or from the mouths of your children, or from the mouths of their descendants from this time on and forever," says the LORD. (Isaiah 59:21)

SUGGESTION TO MY PRAYERS

Here are some Scripture-based prayers, paraphrased and personalized which my husband and I pray regularly for our children:

May the Spirit of the Lord rest upon _____—the Spirit of wisdom and of understanding, the Spirit of counsel and of power, the Spirit of knowledge and of the fear of the Lord. . . . (Isaiah 11:2).

Thank you Lord that you know the plans you have for _____ . . . plans to prosper and not to harm, plans to give _____ hope and a future. Thank you that when we call upon you and come and pray to you, you listen. When we seek you, we find you . . .
(Jeremiah 29:11-13)

Enable your servants _____ to speak your word with great boldness (Acts 4:29b).

FIVE

Praying for Parents and Other Relatives

THEN THE LORD SAID to Noah, "Come into the ark, you and all your household, because I have seen that you are righteous before Me in this generation."

(Genesis 7:1, NKJV)

When God told Noah to go into the ark, his entire family of eight was included; *all* were spared in the flood.

When Rahab the harlot hid the spies in Jericho, she was offered protection from Joshua's invasion of her city—she and *all her father's family*. (See Joshua 2:12-19.)

When Zacchaeus, a wealthy tax collector, met Jesus he agreed to repay all he had acquired through cheating. Jesus responded, "Today *salvation has come to this house,* because this man, too, is a son of Abraham. For the Son of Man came to seek and to save what was lost" (Luke 19: 9, 10).

"Believe in the Lord Jesus, and you will be saved, you *and your household,*" Paul told the jailer who wanted to kill himself because an earthquake had freed all the inmates in his prison. The Bible says Paul told him about the Lord and then *"the whole family* was filled with joy, because they had come to believe in God." (See Acts 16:25-34.)

Cornelius, the first Gentile believer, accepted salvation when Peter preached in his home, and his *relatives and close friends* also believed and were baptized. (See Acts 11:4-18.)

Lydia became Paul's first European convert, and she *and her household* were saved and baptized. (See Acts 16:13-15.)

SALVATION: GOD'S PLAN

Salvation for the entire household was God's plan— and it continues to be his plan—for your family and for mine. The door to Noah's ark was a door of rescue and salvation for his family. Today, Jesus Christ is the door to the ark of salvation through whom our loved ones will be saved. Our part is to pray them into the ark.

The Bible offers much encouragement to believers who are standing in faith for family members to come into the ark:

> Therefore know that the Lord your God, He is God, the faithful God who keeps covenant and mercy for a thousand generations with those who love Him and keep His commandments. (Deuteronomy 7:9, NKJV)

> "... On My menservants and on My maidservants I will pour out My Spirit in those days.... And it shall come to pass that whoever calls on the name of the Lord shall be saved." (Joel 2:29, 32, NKJV)

> The Lord is not slack concerning His promise, as some count slackness, but is longsuffering toward us, not

willing that any should perish but that all should come to repentance. (2 Peter 3:9, NKJV)

HONORING OUR PARENTS

The Ten Commandments clearly teach that God places high priority on honoring parents. Yet we read in the Bible of struggles between children and parents: Jonathan with King Saul; Samson with his parents; Esau with Rebecca; Absalom with David; Jacob with ten of his sons.

In the ideal biblical pattern, parents train their children in the ways of the Lord, and the children obey and honor their parents by following their godly example. (See Ephesians 6:1-4.) But the effects of selfishness and rebellion so often mar child-parent relationships. Such problems are the product of sin, and Jesus is the only solution to the sin problem.

My friend May suffered over the relationship with her father, who repeatedly slapped and kicked his four children and two stepchildren, often shouting obscenities at them. He made excuses for his violent temper because his own father had deserted him when he was a baby, so he never had a role model or father figure in his life. The only time he ever showed May any affection was when he kissed her goodbye as she left for college.

May married her college sweetheart. By the time she had three children, she was horrified to realize she was treating them just as her dad had treated her—physically and verbally abusing them. She hated herself for it but couldn't seem to stop.

When May cried out for help, a friend led her to Jesus. She released her anger to the Lord, asked him to forgive her, and he filled the void in her heart with his love. Next she asked each of her children to forgive her for all the times she'd hurt them and lashed out at them in rage.

RECONCILIATION WITH PARENTS

Desiring her parents to know the love of the Lord she had received, May began praying fervently for them. About that time her mother phoned with some bad news: May's alcoholic father was divorcing her mom after forty-three years of marriage. Now she had to ask the Lord to help her deal with new feelings of resentment against her dad.

While attending a retreat, May went to the speaker for prayer to ask God to heal her wounds and resentments against her father. She forgave him. Then she had a vision of the heavens opening and Jesus, bathed in flames and light, appeared and spoke to her: "I want to introduce you to my Father."

In the vision May told the Heavenly Father, "I'm sorry, but I don't understand you." Immediately she felt inundated with God's love. All the hurts of forty years seemed to wash away as she heard herself saying over and over, "Dad, my Dad, he didn't mean to . . . he didn't mean to hurt us . . ."

She went to visit her elderly father and told him, "I've forgiven you for all the times you mistreated me. I've been praying for you for years now, and I can say tonight I really love you. I release you from all my judgments, and I thank you for what you gave me materially. Dad, if you do nothing else in your lifetime, please tell each one of us kids at least once that you love us."

The father's eyes filled with tears as he studied her face and hung onto her words, occasionally nodding in agreement. "Thank you for coming to see me," he said. "I guess I need to think through what you've said. But I do love you—it's just hard for me to show it."

Before the week was over he called May's sister for the first time in twenty-five years and talked for an hour. He ended the conversation by saying those three wonderful words, "I love you."

"I'm sorry he lives four hundred miles away," May told me. "If he lived nearer, our relationship would be even closer, but the Lord has truly brought reconciliation and healing between us. I also have a new appreciation for my Heavenly Father since I've forgiven my earthly father."

May's mother nearly had a mental breakdown over the divorce. She came to visit May for three weeks and went with her to several Bible studies. One night at a prayer meeting she accepted the Lord, then eagerly began to read the Bible. May was then able to minister to her mother concerning the rejection and loneliness she was feeling after the divorce. Although the circumstances were painful, mother and daughter were brought closer together through prayer.

CHILD LEADS PARENT TO JESUS

When Jenny gave her heart to the Lord a dozen years ago, she longed for her elderly mother to know Jesus too. She and her husband agreed that they would show love and forgiveness toward her at every opportunity.

"I hadn't been a reliable or trustworthy daughter so I had to prove myself, so to speak," she told me. "Mother had to see that Jesus Christ had really changed my life before she would be willing to follow my example."

At Jenny's urging, the mother enrolled in a Bible course with her. "During those weeks we grew closer spiritually," Jenny related. "After my father died, she began to lean on me more and more, allowing me to help her make decisions both big and little."

A short time later Jenny's mother committed her life to the Lord, and the two were able to relate to one another in a fresh and deeper way. When the mother faced open heart surgery, they both realized she might not live through it.

"The day before her surgery I spent the entire day with her in her hospital room. I asked if she had any unfinished business with God, or if she needed to forgive anyone. For hours Mom unburdened her heart. Each time a new topic of hurt surfaced we stopped and prayed about it.

"She talked through some very pain-filled areas of her life, some regrets and some disappointments. As I prayed over each area she and I both experienced a supernatural joy—unlike anything we had ever known."

Her mother lived fifteen more months after the surgery. God answered Jenny's prayers by giving her a support group of strong Christian friends during that time, and by providing good medical care for her mom which was covered by insurance.

"It is never too late for someone to come into the kingdom," Jenny declared. "Though my mother waited until her extremely late years to accept Jesus, she finally was won through love and acceptance and extensive prayer. It built my confidence in God's faithfulness to his Word."

ATTITUDE CHANGED THROUGH PRAYER

Bible teacher and missionary John Garlock shares a recent answer to prayer for his ninety-two-year-old mother:

I was heartsick when the doctor told me my elderly mother would have to have her hip surgery completely done over. After breaking her hip in a fall on the shower room floor in the nursing home where she lived, Mom had endured days of agony recovering from the implantation of an artificial part in the joint. Now the implant had failed.

What bothered me even more than the prospect of her physical pain was what it would do to her state of mind. A lifelong Christian, for years a compassionate missionary in Africa, she had been something of a holy terror in the hospital during her first ordeal.

She seemed angry with everyone, God included. For a woman her age she was actually violent at times, and had to endure restraints on her arms. Now, after only a few painful days back in the nursing home, she must reenter the hospital over Christmas and go through it all again.

But I can report (with some amazement) that her second experience was so different from the first that you would hardly believe she was the same woman. Same doctor, same hospital wing, same operation, same personnel she had been almost cursing before. But somehow everything was different. No more screaming. No more throwing things around the room. I soon realized it was prayer that made the difference.

During her first operation I was extremely busy and my wife, who is stalwart in prayer, was out of the country. I alerted only a few of her praying friends, but our main focus was on her physical problem.

Then the second time around we enlisted more praying people who know and love my mother. We prayed for her peace of mind; we rebuked influences that would disrupt her Christian testimony; we believed for a happier, more optimistic attitude.

The results proved, for me at least, the dynamic power of prayer. Her emotional and physical recoveries were so much easier! Her understanding and acceptance were so much better! We could actually reason with her.

At this writing, only three weeks after the second surgery, she is doing well, gaining strength, and already walking a bit every day with the aid of a walker. The anger is gone. It's as near a laboratory test as one could have in "measuring" the effectiveness of prayer. The only significant variable was *focused prayer*. And what a difference!

RELEASING OUR LOVED ONES

When it is God's time to take our loved ones, we must be willing to release them into the Lord's hands. Elizabeth is a friend who was the only one beside her mother's bed as she lay dying. Three times as she seemed to be struggling to breathe her last, Elizabeth prayed for life to spring back into her. Each time her mother regained her strength.

Finally she whispered, "Elizabeth Ann, release me and

let me go to my Lord." Elizabeth realized it was her time to go. When she stopped praying for life to come back, the mother slipped peacefully into death with a smile.

PRAYING FOR OTHER RELATIVES

At a family Christmas gathering, an eighty-one-year-old grandmother was complaining that her life was useless. "But Granny," her thirty-one-year-old grandson protested, "you can go out of this world in a blaze of glory as an intercessor!"

It got her attention. "I don't know how to intercede for others," she said to her daughter-in-law. "Would you teach me?" That night she had her first prayer lesson as they spread out a world map on the table, got out the Bible, and began to pray over various countries and for missionaries they knew.

They also made a list of relatives for whom she could pray. This "useless granny" is launched on a whole new adventure that can change her perspective on life.

Senior citizens can be valuable prayer warriors in their later years—praying for their family, friends and missionaries, and for God's will to be accomplished here on earth. And the prayer improves their own sense of well-being as an added bonus.

Before my mother died she prayed daily, usually with both hands raised, saying, "Lord, my ten fingers represent my ten grandchildren. . . ." Then she would name them and pray, "Accomplish your perfect will in their lives today, Lord. Give them wisdom beyond their experience."

Since her death, I've taken up the charge to pray for my

nieces and nephews. One of them wrote me recently to say he has made a commitment to the Lord, and is seeking God's call on his life. My children join me in praying for their cousins on both sides of the family, and we expect to see all of them come into the ark.

A woman in Toronto told me the Lord has commissioned her to pray for her husband's forty-eight nieces and nephews. For some of those people, she may well be the only one praying for them to find the Lord.

Of course, the need for prayer includes more than just praying for a person to come to saving knowledge of Christ. As the Holy Spirit gives direction, we should pray for our loved ones' protection, provision, good health, guidance, and spiritual growth. No doubt we will run short of time and energy before we run short of things to pray about.

PRAYER FOR SIBLINGS

Chrissy sleepily answered the phone late one night and heard her older brother's voice on the line. "Sis, I just invited Jesus into my life!" he shouted. "I'm saved! The preacher said to tell someone immediately, so I knew I had to call you because you've prayed for me for so long."

The praying sister sat speechless with the phone in her hand. This brother of hers—the one who had mocked and screamed at her at their mother's funeral when she tried to share Jesus with him—the one who had broken up a pastor's home to marry his third and current wife—this rebel was calling to say he'd accepted Jesus. She could hardly believe it!

Why is it when our loved ones are saved in answer to prayers we've prayed for years, we are always surprised?

Could it be that we secretly doubt whether our prayers will really change anything? Or that we've written off the person as hopeless?

When Raymond's brother was dying, he stood by the hospital bed and said boldly, "Henry, I've prayed for you for years. I'm tired of you cursing the Lord I serve. It's time you accepted him and all he has done for you! You could very well die tonight; where would you spend eternity?"

Henry acknowledged his need for God and asked Jesus into his heart right then. Finally, after fifteen years, Raymond saw his prayers for his brother dramatically answered just a few days before Henry died.

A DREAM AND A PRAYER

Tillie prayed constantly for her niece, Lisa, who was hooked on prescription drugs, her life in total chaos. "I asked God to deliver her from the bondage of drug addiction," she told me. "One day Lisa fell into my arms crying because she'd dreamed Jesus returned and she was left behind. I prayed aloud for her as she sobbed in my arms.

"Then I took her by the shoulders, looked her in the face and asked, 'What are you going to do about your life? Is the devil going to win, or are you going to turn around and let Jesus help you?'"

Lisa asked her aunt to write out a prayer for her to learn to say every morning as she drove to work. Tillie did, and she also encouraged her to read her Bible and to pray on her own.

"I continually held her before the Lord, praying for Christians her age to befriend her," Tillie told me. "A year later she began attending church with a friend of hers, and the Holy Spirit began a work in her. When her mother underwent serious surgery, Lisa's faith remained steadfast; she did not go back to her drug habit. God does answer prayer!"

PRAYING FOR THE ELDERLY

Most of us have someone in our family who is elderly and will die within a few short years. How do we pray for them? When my mother was approaching death she often quoted 2 Timothy 4:7, 8. We could take those verses and paraphrase them into a prayer for an elderly loved one:

Lord, help my dad to fight the good fight of faith and to finish the course you've appointed for him. Thank you that a crown of righteousness awaits him—a crown which you, the righteous judge, will award to him when you call him home. Until then, comfort him with your Word, your presence, and the encouragement of family members and friends. In Jesus' name, Amen.

In asking others with elderly Christian relatives how they pray for them, here are some replies:

"I pray that God's will and purpose will be accomplished in their lives."

"I pray that they will not be in pain or confused in their thinking."

"I pray for God's mercy on them . . . for them to be comforted and not depressed. Sometimes I do warfare against the spirits of oppression that cause them to be overwhelmed."

"The Holy Spirit often prompts me to write a short note to them or call them on the phone to let them know that I love them and that I am praying for God's best for them."

"Sometimes like the Apostle Paul, if I discern an evil spirit acting up in them, I speak to it, 'I command you foul spirit of (name what God shows me it is) to come out of (name the person) and leave him/her alone in the name of Jesus Christ of Nazareth.'"

"I pray for Jesus to heal them of their infirmities just as he did when on earth so they can die without being afflicted with disease."

"I pray they will not be tormented."

"I pray a prayer of release: 'Lord God, I place my loved one (name) in your hands. Do as it seems good and right in your plan and purpose, but stay the devil's plan and scheme.'"

"I pray that my elderly father, like Moses at his death, will not have eyes that are weak nor strength that is gone." (See Deuteronomy 34:7.)

"I thank the Lord for the Christian heritage passed on to me through that relative."

"When my mother was just a few days from death, every night my husband and I went to her bedside and spoke aloud, 'Father, into your hands we commit Mom's spirit.'"

Prayer for Parents Who Are Old

Lord, it hurts so much to see my parents grow feeble and suffer with infirmities. Heavenly Father, I commit them into your loving care. Only you know the number of their days. I thank you that because they know Jesus, they are assured of eternal life with him—where there will be no aching, deformed bodies or minds affected by disease. Give me the patience, kindness, and gentleness I need to respond in love to the many demands made on me in caring for them.

I thank you for them, Lord. You knew exactly the parents I needed. I now release them from my expectations! Touch their bodies with your healing power. Keep them from feeling lonely, unwanted, and useless. I praise you for my parents, Lord, and what they have meant to me. Now in their latter years, may I be to them what they need. I come asking this in the name of your blessed Son, Jesus. Amen.

For Unsaved Parents

Lord, I'm grieved because my parents haven't accepted Jesus as Savior. I know it is not your will that any perish. I stand in the gap in prayer for them, bringing them to your throne of grace and mercy. God, have mercy on them. May the Holy Spirit woo them to Jesus. God, grant them repentance that they may escape from the trap of the devil (2 Peter 3:9, 2 Timothy 2:25).

Prayer for Other Relatives

Lord, you rescued me from the raging storm, and because you did, I have faith that my relatives can be rescued, too. Lord, just as you spared Lot and his family through the intercession of his uncle, Abraham, I now ask that you do that for my family. Because it's not your will that any perish, I hang my hope, faith, and trust in your strong right arm reaching out to save. Lord, send harvesters into the field to talk to them about you. Use me as an instrument of peace and reconciliation in my family. In Jesus' name, Amen.

Warfare

I come against unbelief and all the powers of darkness holding captive the thoughts and minds of my parents, _____. Because of Jesus' blood shed, I use his authority in applying this Scripture to those strongholds: "Casting down imaginations, and every high thing that exalteth itself against the knowledge of God, and bringing into captivity every thought to the obedience of Christ" (2 Corinthians 10:5 KJV).

Prayer for Parents Still Living

Thank you, Lord, for the parents you have given me. Help me to honor them in the way you intended for parents to be honored by their children. I admit there are times when I've been disappointed in them and by them. I've failed them too. Let your love flow through us, one to another. Help us to forgive one another just as Christ in God forgives us.

Lord, grant them repentance leading to the knowledge of the truth. Give them strength, wisdom, and improved health. I ask in Jesus' name, Amen.

SIX

Praying for Friends and Neighbors

BUT A CERTAIN SAMARITAN, as he journeyed, came where he was. And when he saw him, he had compassion. So he went to him and bandaged his wounds, pouring on oil and wine; and he set him on his own animal, brought him to an inn, and took care of him.

(Luke 10:33, 34)

The April sun was quickly sinking as my friend Gloria and I walked along the white sandy beach near my home, watching the pounding waves. When they occasionally lapped over our feet we jumped from the shock of the cold, laughing like small schoolgirls.

We don't often see each other because three hundred miles separate us, yet we keep our friendship warm by frequent phone calls and occasional visits.

On this particular afternoon we began to reminisce.

"Glo, you visit so seldom—being tied down with your family business—but we always seem to do our best praying here at the beach."

"We sure do," she agreed, brushing the sand off her feet

with a towel. "God's really been faithful to answer, hasn't he?" Stopping to sit on our beach towel, we began to recall some of our answered prayers for Gloria and her family.

1 For God to remove from her daughter's life a woman who had a detrimental influence on her. He did.
2. For her daughter and son-in-law to find a house of their own. After living with Gloria for over eight years, they found a house just right for them, in just the neighborhood they desired.
3. For her daughter (her only child) to have a baby, which was the couple's great desire. After almost thirteen years of marriage her daughter had a son. She nearly died after the birth, but God restored her health, again after much prayer.
4. For her daughter and son-in-law to grow spiritually. They matured so rapidly, her son-in-law was soon teaching the adult Sunday School class of the new church they joined.
5. For her family business to continue to provide financially for them. The mortgage was finally paid off as she and her daughter worked together in the business.
6. For Gloria's safety as she took trips with various Christian mission groups—to Africa, China, Israel.
7. For her own health to be restored after she had to be hospitalized for exhaustion.

Then Gloria shared her most recent prayer request: for her business—which has been in the family more than forty years—to sell. It was a big step for this widow to take. But sitting there on the beach we began to pray with expectancy, because we'd seen God answer prayer so faithfully over the years. In his timing, I'll log the answer to this in my prayer diary as "mission accomplished."

BRINGING FRIENDS TO JESUS

Jesus yearns for us to bring our friends to him. Notice how he honored the faith of the four men who took their paralyzed friend on a stretcher to him to be healed. When they couldn't get into the house where Jesus was ministering because of the crowds, they didn't give up.

They found another way . . . the roof.

Yes, they climbed up on the rooftop, dug a hole large enough to get the stretcher through, and lowered the man into the room right in front of Jesus.

It took time, effort, and ingenuity, but they didn't give up until they got their friend to the Master. The determination and faith of four friends, teamed with Jesus' willingness to heal, restored the paralyzed man to perfect health.

When a crisis hits, we need to press in until our friends are touched by Jesus, not giving up when the way seems blocked. But we also need to pray for our friends on a regular basis, not just in emergencies.

FAITHFUL STRETCHER CARRIERS

Our friends' son, Scott, suffered an emotional illness due to a chemical imbalance. After hospitalization, he returned home to recuperate for many months.

Close family friends prayed faithfully and with persistence. In time his health improved, he got a job, and was engaged to be married. A year later, though, the job ran out, his engagement was broken, and Scott was back at home with the same medical diagnosis.

Upon learning about it, I admitted with shame that I had not been praying as much for him, once he had secured a good job and met a girl who loved him. I had become slack in my commitment to stand in the gap with the family.

Prayer groups were alerted to pray for his healing. In a sense we who prayed were "stretcher carriers" who took Scott to Jesus.

He has since recovered from the second bout—thanks to the Lord's intervention—and is in another job, picking up the pieces of his life. I learned a valuable lesson, however. We need to pray for our friends and for their family members consistently.

Each of us has a unique set of friends, a circle of influence, that no other person on earth has. Have we considered that as a prayer challenge? A prayer privilege?

From time to time my children bring me names of young people for whose salvation they want me to pray. As a result, my prayer list constantly grows and changes.

WHO IS MY NEIGHBOR?

Jesus gave us two great commands: to love the Lord with all our hearts, souls, strength, and minds, and to love our neighbor as ourselves. (See Luke 10:27.)

Then to answer the question "Who is my neighbor?" Jesus related a parable: A traveling Jewish man attacked by thieves was robbed, beaten, and left by the roadside to die. Soon a priest passed him by, followed by a Levite—both "men of the cloth" who were too occupied with their own affairs to help the traveler. But a Samaritan stopped, bandaged the man's wounds, and took him to an inn-keeper, offering to pay any extra expenses incurred in his care.

Obviously, the Samaritan—a member of an ethnic minority group hated by the Jews—was the one who saw the wounded traveler as his neighbor, and acted accordingly. Jesus said, "Go and do likewise" (Luke 10:37).

How can we apply that in our prayer lives? For one thing most of us have contact with friends or neighbors who have been robbed and "beaten" by the devil and his evil forces. In effect, they've been left to die without a Savior. We must care enough to stop, minister to their needs, and take them to Jesus, the Innkeeper, who is preparing a place for us for eternity.

ONE-ON-ONE COMMITMENT

Doreen was deeply concerned as she watched her next-door neighbor Roseanne plunge deeper and deeper into depression after her mother died. Having been deserted by her husband, Roseanne had depended on her mother to help raise her three children, and had counted on her for companionship.

Though she had prayed for Roseanne for years, Doreen felt it was now time to get spiritually involved in her life. She offered to go to her home on Thursday nights and teach Roseanne some basic Bible principles that would help her deal with depression.

Every Thursday evening for three years, Doreen sat at

Roseanne's kitchen table, and over cookies and tea offered her hope and encouragement through God's Word. At first she sensed Roseanne only tolerated her because of her own loneliness. But gradually the spiritual seeds she planted began to take root and bear fruit. Roseanne's depression lifted and she committed her life to the Lord.

One night Roseanne's teenage son, Nathan, took some angel dust, and in his drug-induced state had a vision of hell. In the midst of flashes of fire and piercing screams, he distinctly heard a voice say, "This is where you are going, but you have a choice."

He ran to his mother because he knew she had the answer. "Help me! I don't want to go to hell," he pleaded.

Roseanne took him to church where the pastor prayed with him. Nathan returned home and destroyed all his drugs, and over the next two months the pastor counseled and prayed with Nathan. Soon his mind was completely restored.

Nathan later married and got a job. While working as a carpenter, he completed a Bible correspondence course and today is in full-time ministry.

At a neighborhood farewell party held for him, Nathan shared with everyone how Jesus had drastically changed his life and had called him into ministry. Many non-Christians at the party were deeply moved by his testimony—all because eleven years earlier his mother's neighbor was willing to sacrifice some time every week teaching her about the Bible.

What if Doreen had quit in just one year? Or in two? Persistent and faithful, she spent three years going next door until Roseanne was firmly established in her faith. It isn't always convenient or easy to spend ourselves for the kingdom. But it fulfills Jesus' command to "love your neighbor as yourself."

A HUNGRY NEIGHBOR

In some cases it's the hungry neighbor who reaches out for help. Carol and Pat, both of whom are Christians, live on the same street and have children close in age who attend the same schools. They became casual friends, helping one another with carpooling and babysitting.

But Pat sensed that Carol's relationship with the Lord seemed much more vital than her own, and she was hungry to know God more intimately. A friend of hers had gone to Carol for counseling and had had prayer to receive the baptism of the Holy Spirit. So Pat began asking questions.

Carol shared Scriptures with Pat, tried to answer her questions, and prayed, asking the Holy Spirit to reveal his truth to her. She also began praying for Pat's husband, Robert, an agnostic who constantly berated Pat for believing in God.

One day Carol's phone rang. "This is Pat ... I'm ready to receive the Holy Spirit. Can you come pray with me?"

Carol went to her house and they had a prayer meeting in Pat's living room. She instantly received the Holy Spirit and began to praise the Lord in tongues as a deep joy engulfed her.

Four months later Pat's husband gave up his agnosticism and accepted Jesus as Lord of his life. Within a few weeks Carol's phone rang again ... this time a call to pray with Robert to receive the Holy Spirit. His experience was much like Pat's; he instantly began to speak in tongues as he lifted praises to the God he had once ridiculed. Today he's a volunteer for a Bible distribution organization.

Now Carol and Pat meet for prayer once a week to pray specifically for the neighborhood, for their children, and for the schools. Carol already had the habit of praying over the neighborhood every time she went jogging, and Pat had been driving around their area to pray when she went to get her children from school; they've simply joined forces.

Recently, at a social function, Pat met a woman who inquired what section of the city she lived in. When Pat told her the woman replied, "That's a very safe neighborhood. I used to work at City Hall, and I remember noticing in the statistics that your area has the lowest crime rate in the city."

Here are two neighbors praying together waging their own war on crime—it's a war in the heavenlies!

NEIGHBORHOOD PRAYER PLAN

Mapping a prayer plan for the neighborhood is an idea shared by Theresa Mulligan, editor of *Breakthrough*, a newsletter for intercessors.

When she moved to her new neighborhood, Theresa learned the names and as much as she could about the twelve other families who lived on her cul-de-sac. Her purpose: to pray for the salvation of each household on the street.

When she met Doris, another Christian on the block who had been praying for a Christian to move into the neighborhood, they agreed to take a prayer walk and pray in front of each house. At the first house they stood holding hands in agreement and prayed, "Lord, bring your love and power to this house—to Colonel and Mrs. H. and their daughters."

"Around the street we paraded that morning, the excitement growing as we went . . . to the young couple hoping for a child, to the elderly widow suffering from arthritis, to the couple who drank too much, to the Jewish family, and so on. As we prayed, faith spread under our feet. We felt his presence and pleasure upon us," Theresa writes.

"Before long we heard that the Colonel was being transferred overseas. His wife disappeared to another part of the country to say goodbye to relatives. When she returned, Doris's family invited her to a farewell dinner. That night the Colonel's wife confided to Doris that while visiting her sister she had received the Lord..

"Soon other reports reached our ears . . . the teenage daughter of the Jewish family had made a commitment to the Lord, the arthritic woman had received Jesus at a Women's Aglow meeting. The same thing happened to the college-age daughter of the alcoholic parents when Doris took her to a fellowship of young people."[1]

Even after Theresa moved away, she kept receiving reports of others in that cul-de-sac becoming Christians.

For those who want to begin praying for their neighbors, Theresa gives some guidelines:

1. Ask God to show you what strategy he wants you to use in reaching out to your neighbors—get-acquainted meals, coffee klatschs, or similar social gatherings.

2. Ask God to open up opportunities for building friendships and performing services for your neighbors. Think creatively!

3. Ask God to show you any areas where perhaps you need to be reconciled with one or more of your neighbors. Confess any sins the Holy Spirit reveals in this area.

4. Search Scripture for a special word for each neighbor and expect God to speak to your heart specifically.

5. After any neighbors commit their lives to Jesus, be willing to continue to walk with them as they are nurtured and grow in the Word and in the Body of Christ.[2]

Ask the Lord to show you your own neighborhood from his perspective. Those who live on your street, in your apartment complex, or in your dormitory offer you opportunities for prayer and for bringing needy ones to Jesus.

Usually the "Good Samaritan Principle" is good to follow. That is, those most likely to respond to prayer and friendship are the bleeding ones, so look for them. Develop a sensitivity to discern who the hurting ones are—despite an outer facade they may try to hide behind.

Outside your door are unlimited adventures in prayer just waiting for an intercessor to take up the challenge.

Prayer

Father, thank you for the people you bring into my life—not by accident, but by divine appointment! Help me to be sensitive to your leading in how to pray for the friends and neighbors you've given me. Thank you for the opportunity to be a "stretcher carrier" in bringing them to you.

Lord, help me to be more like the Good Samaritan—not so much concerned about the cost, but rejoicing in the rewards of having others come to know you personally. I'm so glad someone cared enough to share the Good News with me when I needed to know your love. Thank you, in Jesus' name, Amen.

SEVEN

Praying for Enemies and Strangers

BLESS THOSE WHO CURSE YOU, pray for those who mistreat you. (Luke 6:28)

I urge . . . that requests, prayers, intercession and thanksgiving be made for everyone. . . . This is good, and pleases God our Savior, who wants all men to be saved and to come to a knowledge of the truth.

(1 Timothy 2:1, 3, 4)

When Stephen, an early church disciple, was being stoned to death after the Jews falsely accused him of blasphemy, he prayed, "Lord, do not hold this sin against them" (Acts 7:60). By this prayer, Stephen released the stone-throwers from his own judgment and committed them into God's hands.

Saul of Tarsus, a well-known persecutor of Christians, stood nearby observing and approving of the violence. But Stephen's courageous witness had an eternal impact on him, and thus on the entire Christian world. Shortly after Stephen's death Saul had a personal encounter with

Jesus, received the Holy Spirit, and became the leading apostle in the early church. What a powerful example of the impact praying for one's enemy can have.

SANDPAPER PEOPLE

Some of us are extremely reluctant to pray for those outside our realm of family or friends. We don't know these people well, and some of those we do know, we just plain don't like.

Does it seem to you that God places many sandpaper people in your life—those abrasive ones who bring out the very worst in you? A controlling, gossipy neighbor . . . a teacher with a grudge against you or your child . . . a boss who is out to axe you or your spouse . . . an unbearable coworker. . . . The list goes on.

Today some of us are "stoned" with words by persecutors close to us—family, friends, and enemies. We can choose to forgive them, release them from our judgment, and continue to pray and believe for their salvation. Or we can remain chained to them by our resentments and judgments—and block our own prayers. (See Matthew 6:14, 15; 7:2; Mark 11:25.)

"BLESS HIM REAL GOOD, LORD"

Joy had a hard decision to make concerning a man who constantly berated her son, thus wounding her. She always sat in the parents' cheering section when her son Don played basketball for the junior high team.

This other parent who attended the games, however,

seemed to "have it in" for her son. Whenever Don made the slightest mistake, the man would scream, "Hey, Don, Mr. Stupid . . . got brains in your feet, kid?"

Once Joy's husband became so angry he left the game, knowing if he stayed he would punch the man in the face. Finally, he stopped going to watch Don play at all.

"My son was being humiliated. My husband was angry. I could think of nothing to do but pray," Joy shared with me. "I remembered a Scripture verse that says we should bless those who curse us—and that's what this man was doing. So I prayed, 'Lord, in the name of Jesus, I forgive that man. I ask you to bless him. Bless him real good, Lord. Just keep on blessing him. Amen.'"

The next weekend Joy went alone to the out-of-town game. The man who always yelled at her son saw her. "Mind if I sit here?" he asked, turning into the row where she was. "Other parents from our team will probably sit in this section, too."

Joy hesitated. Let him sit beside her? Was he serious? Then she remembered her prayer.

"Go ahead," she said, nodding her approval.

As the game progressed Joy noticed the man was acting quite differently. Only once did he let go with a string of critical remarks about Don's performance. Turning to Joy he said, "Oh, I'm sorry. I've got to learn to keep my mouth shut and to control my temper."

The man she had prayed for and asked God to bless was now apologizing for yelling at Don!

"When Jesus taught us to bless those who persecute us, he knew it was to bring about a change—both in us and in them," Joy told me. The results: the man eventually stopped yelling at any of the players, and at out-of-town games he became Joy's protector.

LOVE YOUR ENEMIES

Frank, a friend of mine who teaches Bible studies for prisoners, shared with me his experience of struggling to live his own lesson while teaching his men about loving your enemies. He had been promised a promotion on his job and was looking forward to the challenge of the new assignment, as well as to the extra money for his family's needs. Then he learned he had an "enemy" to contend with.

Another engineer in his office did everything to discredit his qualifications and got the position himself. Of course Frank was very disappointed. For a few days he nursed his hurt, but he knew full-well Jesus' command:

> "Love your enemies and pray for those who persecute you, that you may be sons of your Father in heaven.... And when you stand praying, if you hold anything against anyone, forgive him, so that your Father in heaven may forgive you your sins."
>
> (Matthew 5:44, 45; Mark 11:25)

So Frank chose to forgive the man and began to pray for the coworker who had jockeyed the job away from him, because that man was now his supervisor. Months passed. One day the new boss called all his employees in and announced: "After twenty-seven years of marriage, my wife and I are getting a divorce. Please pray for me."

That gave Frank the opening he'd been waiting for. He shared with his boss how thirteen years earlier he had been divorced from his wife, but in the three years they were separated each of them had accepted Jesus; they had since reconciled and remarried.

"God wants to restore marriages," Frank told him. "I'll be praying for God's best in your life."

As we talked about it, my friend admitted that if he had not forgiven and begun praying for the man, he could not have responded with compassion or offered him hope in the midst of a failing marriage. But Frank became his encourager, and he and his wife prayed for this man and his estranged wife. Frank's wife's prayer group also joined the prayer effort, though the people concerned were strangers to most of those in the group. Some months later their prayers were answered when the couple reconciled. Frank's boss now confides in him and considers him a friend, not an enemy.

We must have clean hearts when we approach God's throne in prayer if we want to see our prayers answered, and to have a clean heart we must forgive those who have wronged us.

When someone has offended me I tend to plead, "Oh, God, change this person!" only to find he wants to change me instead. Or I want to scream, "God, take her out of my life!" And he says, "Not until you can love her as I do."

LIFE OUT OF DEATH

Betty, a Bible teacher in Texas, faced the greatest challenge of her Christian walk when her husband was murdered in an armed robbery at the jewelry store where he worked. She lost her husband and her children lost their father just before Christmas that year.

To her dismay, the gunman and two accomplices were brought to trial for aggravated assault, not for murder. Because they never found the murder weapon, the authorities sought to convict the men on the lesser charge.

"I prayed against it, because it seemed so unfair to my husband," Betty related. "Finally the Lord showed me I had to release it and let him manage it his way. I even had to forgive the district attorney who was handling the case. God's plan was to bring life out of death—not death out of death."

Her greater struggle was to forgive Clarence, the man who had so ruthlessly shot her husband in the face at close range. When the suspect was arrested, the newspapers reported he was an ex-convict and a drifter with no family. Yet every time Betty would begin to pray for him, she found herself weeping and praying for his family.

"God gave me the grace to forgive Clarence, and I began to pray for his salvation," she shared. "I went on the witness stand briefly at the trial. After the jury was dismissed Clarence's father came to me with tears streaming down his face and said, 'I'm so sorry for what happened to your family; I hope you can find it in your heart to forgive us. We didn't raise our son to live like this.'

"I was able to tell him, 'I'm a Christian. I've already forgiven your son, and I'm praying for your family.'"

Clarence and the two accomplices are now serving prison terms for their crimes, and a friend of Betty's who works with a prison ministry stays in contact with them. I asked her how she prays for Clarence now.

"I pray he will be given a new heart and new life in Christ, and that it will be a permanent work—not aborted," she replied. "I'm praying that three new men will come out of prison—not the same ones who went in."

FREE FROM INNER PRISONS

Not long ago Betty accompanied a ministry team on a visit to a state prison where one of Clarence's accomplices is serving his time. She shared the experience of her husband's murder and the hardship it had caused, then talked about the "inner prisons" she could have gone into—prisons of anger, despair, and unforgiveness.

"But I have chosen to forgive the men who murdered my husband," she told the prisoners. "I've been set free from those inner prisons. If there's someone you need to forgive, you are in an inner prison; but if you get free from these inner prisons, you'll never come back to one like this."

As she sang a song of forgiveness and prayed for the men, many of them began weeping and several made decisions for Christ. Betty doesn't know whether the accomplice to her husband's murder was in that meeting, but he surely heard about her testimony from the other men.

Here is the song of forgiveness the Lord gave Betty to sing to the prisoners that day. If you are bound in an inner prison of unforgiveness, perhaps you want to pray this prayer yourself:

All the hurts of all the years,
All the pain and all the tears . . .
Father, I forgive it all.
All the failures, all the strife,
Each disappointment in my life . . .
Father, I forgive it all.
Each loss I have sustained,

All the lies and all the shame,
Father, I forgive it all . . .
Yes, Father, I forgive it all.

PRAY FOR STRANGERS

Praying for our enemies can be very difficult because we see their many faults. Sometimes, though, God brings strangers into our lives—people about whom we know nothing—just so we can intercede for them. In both cases we need the Lord's help to overcome our own selfishness and to know how to pray effectively for the person concerned.

I can think of several significant times when I believe God directed me to a certain place or to a particular seat on an airplane because someone needed prayer.

An attractive woman named Brenda, troubled over personal problems, was one of those. Sitting next to me as I was flying back to Florida one evening, she told me she was on her way to her vacation cottage in our area, but had no one meeting her at the airport.

My son and I not only gave her a ride, but went to visit her several times that week to pray for her. I knew the Lord brought Brenda across my path for me to minister to her spiritual needs, but also to become my friend—which she has!

Another time an airline attendant knelt in the aisle next to me and whispered, "Please pray for me. I'm having such problems with my husband—I need help!"

"I'll be glad to pray for you," I answered. "But how did you know I'm a Christian?"

"A man in the back of the plane is reading a book filled

with scriptures. He said you wrote it and gave it to him while waiting in the Atlanta airport. I need prayer right now."

Grasping her hand, I prayed softly for the Lord to intervene in her marriage, to meet her husband's need, and to give her peace. "Thank you, Jesus—Amen," I finished. She smiled and squeezed my hand. "Thank you so much," she said, then went on with her work.

We almost never know the end of the matter in such situations, but it is gratifying to know we've done something to help the stranger God brings across our path—even at times when it's not convenient.

Jesus told us to pray for laborers to be sent into his harvest (Luke 10:2)—and sometimes we may be the harvesters. I believe as we are faithful to minister to people in this way, God is faithful to send strangers across the paths of our own loved ones to minister to them.

DIVINE APPOINTMENT

While driving home from some radio interviews one day last summer, I felt an inner leading to stop and shop for a large purse I needed for an impending trip.

Two clerks were managing the small outlet shop alone. There were no other customers, so both of them helped me. "I need a large purse, big enough to hold my Bible and my notes on a book I'm writing," I explained.

They began asking questions about the book. "It's a book on how to pray for your family and friends," I answered. "You see, my husband and I prayed together and God brought all three of our children back from their rebellion against him."

"God sent you here today," the younger woman said. "We've just moved here so my husband can attend seminary, and our daughter has withdrawn into a shell because she misses her relatives and friends back home. I need help to know how to deal with this."

I began to pray with that clerk for her little girl, asking God to heal her broken heart, to bring her new friends of his choice, and to help her appreciate the fact that her dad loves the Lord enough to want to study for the ministry.

The other clerk had a rebellious older daughter, so we prayed for her, too. Both of them wept when we finished— delighted that God loved them enough to send along a stranger to pray with them.

As we yield to the Holy Spirit working in our lives, such divine appointments begin to take place with regularity. I sometimes wonder how many marvelous divine appointments I've missed just because I was too insensitive or too caught up in my own problems to recognize them.

"LORD, CHOOSE MY FRIENDS"

My friend, Leona, returned to college to earn her master's degree, though she felt a bit out of place in a classroom of much younger students. "Lord, please choose my new friends for me," she prayed. "I lay down the right to associate only with those whom I happen to like."

Soon Leona realized that a young woman about half her age in her psychology class seemed to shadow her everywhere she went. "She was dreadful," Leona told me. "Virginia was an obnoxious, smart-mouthed, cursing, smoking young divorcee. At first I tried to avoid her, but then I remembered my prayer." Sure enough, God was at work.

"Why don't we carpool to class?" Virginia suggested one day as they walked to the parking lot. "We live close enough to share rides."

Leona reluctantly agreed. She asked her husband and her prayer partner to pray for her on the days they were riding together on the eighty-mile round trip.

On Virginia's day to drive, Leona would open her Bible to read. Sometimes she would read aloud, but after a few minutes Virginia would shout, "Shut that Bible or get out!"

"I knew she was very wounded from her past, and I wanted to see her life healed," Leona told me. "I shared with her how God had strengthened my own troubled marriage, and invited her over for a meal so she could meet my husband."

Leona and Mike often prayed together that Virginia would want to know Jesus personally. Two years passed with no response. But an amazing thing was happening to Leona. She began not only to like her new friend, but to love her.

At last Leona got an urgent call from Virginia. "I need to talk right now," she said. "Please meet me at the Pier Restaurant in half an hour."

After listening to Virginia rehearse her problems for a long time, Leona looked her in the eye and said, "Today's the day. You've heard about my Savior for two years. I told you how he changed my life and Mike's, too. You're so miserable you can't stand things anymore ... give your life to the Lord now! He makes all things new."

Virginia began to shake as if with a chill, but she agreed. "Lord Jesus, come into my life, I need you," she prayed as she wept and poured her heart out to the Lord.

From that day on, no more dirty words spewed from her mouth. She stopped smoking. She became a devoted mother. Best of all, she and her husband remarried and have since helped many other troubled couples.

Such dramatic change may not always be the case, but God had been moving Virginia toward her decision ever since she started carpooling with Leona.

Leona told me, "I've learned that strangers—even obnoxious ones—can be friends in disguise. I'm still asking God to choose my friends for me."

A STRANGER IN THE HOSPITAL

A phone call from my son in Orlando interrupted my busy schedule one morning. "Mom, my roommate's mother is dying of throat cancer in a military hospital near you," he said. "He's recently accepted Jesus, but he's concerned because as far as he knows his mother doesn't know the Lord. Would you go see her and maybe pray for her?"

I revised my schedule for that day and asked my prayer partner, Fran, to join me to visit a stranger in the hospital. Jesus sent his disciples out two by two, and I believe in the partner principle when it comes to ministering to individuals. I knew it would help if one of us could pray while the other talked.

When we walked into the room Beatrice was in such pain she could barely talk. Much of the bone in the left side of her face had been removed, and she was surrounded with tubes and gauges and medical equipment;

she did manage a weak smile when we introduced ourselves.

"Did you know your son Mickey has become a Christian?" I asked, getting right to the point of our visit. "My son rooms with him and has seen such a happy change in him. In fact, Mickey is concerned about your spiritual condition."

"Yes, he told me; I'm glad for him," Beatrice responded. "I used to go to church when I was little but I haven't been in years. I still remember the old hymns we sang. But I've turned my back on God all these years . . . it's just too late . . ."

Fran picked up the conversation, assuring her it was not too late. "Jesus will accept you right where you are," she urged. "Just ask him to forgive your sins and tell him you want to become his child forever."

As Fran read her several Scriptures I prayed silently. Finally Beatrice said, "I'm ready to ask him to forgive me and be my Savior and Lord."

Fran and I listened as she whispered a prayer, "Lord Jesus, please forgive me for my rebellion . . . for running from you. Come live in my heart. I want to be yours."

SHE MADE IT TO HEAVEN

I visited her a few more times, taking her a Bible and some Christian literature. I always prayed aloud before I left. Beatrice grew too weak to talk, but she could still squeeze my hand when I prayed with her.

She died within a few weeks. At the funeral home I met her son Mickey. "She accepted Jesus before she died—I heard her whispered prayer with my own ears," I told him. "She was so happy you've become a Christian."

I'd hardly finished my sentence when an elderly lady spoke up. "Forgive me for listening in, but I'm Beatrice's mother. I taught Sunday school for forty years, and I can't remember a day when I didn't pray for my prodigal child—my only daughter—to come back to the Lord."

"Well, dear, your prayers were answered," I assured her.

"She made it to heaven! She actually accepted Jesus just days before she died!" the woman exclaimed, wiping tears from her eyes. "Thank you, Jesus! Thank you, Lord, for your faithfulness."

I left the funeral home thanking the Lord for the opportunity to be a part of the answer to the prayers of that mother and son. God wants us to carry one another's burdens, even when those "others" are strangers to us.

STRANGERS BY ACCIDENT

Sometimes we pray for strangers when they suddenly pop into our life without warning and we get involved with them, even remotely. Like recently when a pickup pulling a trailer load of lumber turned over in front of us. My friend Janet and I were in the only other car around and we began praying very loudly when we saw the trailer begin to jackknife. Thankfully the two men climbed out of the smashed cab, which resembled a folded accordian, amid our shouts of "Thank you, Jesus."

Sometimes you and I may be the only ones praying when an ambulance whizzes around us or a firetruck sounds an alarm on the way to meet an emergency. The possibilities for interceding for strangers are almost limitless if we but tune our spiritual ears to the activities around us.

PRAYING FOR THOSE WHO SEEM UNLOVABLE

When I asked several Christian friends how they pray for those they find it hard to love I got these answers:

"In the name of Jesus Christ, I bind the spirit of deception that is telling him sin is fun, and I ask God to create a hunger for God and his Word in his heart. I bind a manipulative spirit, a lying spirit, a spirit of confusion, or whatever else I perceive to be the root of the problem; then I ask the Lord to release peace and harmony into that person's life."

"I ask God to pour his love into my heart according to Romans 5:5 so that I can love with his love."

"I ask God to bless the one who seems bent on making my life so miserable. There must be a reason for her to react to me in such an irritating manner. Perhaps there is a home problem, or a financial struggle, or a health problem, or even a poor self-image because of hurts in her past. Sometimes the Holy Spirit will show me specifically to pray for her family members, or her finances, or health. Other times, he gives me ideas for ways to respond more kindly when she lashes out."

"I often thank God in advance for the change he will bring about: 'Thank you, Lord, that my elderly neighbor will come into the kingdom, because it is not your will that she perish. I realize she tries to control our neighborhood because she is in the kingdom of darkness. Open her eyes to the light of Jesus Christ. I thank you that she will acknowledge Jesus as Lord before her death.' ''

Prayer

Lord, keep me sensitive about *how* to pray for those in my life whom I don't particularly like. Help me remember that Jesus washed his friend Judas's feet, knowing he would betray him. Help me follow Jesus' example who, when he was reviled, reviled not again. May I be willing to stand in prayer for those I associate with on a regular basis, as well as for the strangers you bring across my path. I ask in Jesus' name, Amen.

For those who feel threatened by any person of violence:

A Prayer of David

Rescue me, O Lord, from evil men; protect me from men of violence, who devise evil plans in their hearts. . . . Keep me, O Lord, from the hands of the wicked; protect me from men of violence who plan to trip my feet. . . . do not grant the wicked their desires, O Lord; do not let their plans succeed. (Based on Psalm 140:1, 2, 4, 8.)

EIGHT

The Forgiveness Factor

FOR IF YOU FORGIVE MEN when they sin against you, your heavenly Father will also forgive you. But if you do not forgive men their sins, your Father will not forgive your sins. (Matthew 6:14, 15)

Our pastor, Peter Lord, finished teaching the weekly Bible study in our home one Sunday evening. Upon returning to his car, he found this terse note from our neighbor stuck on the windshield: "You parked on my grass and I don't like it. Don't do it again."

Pastor Lord quickly scribbled a response on the back of the note and put it in our neighbor's door. He wrote, "You are right. I am wrong. Forgive me; I won't do it again. Pastor Peter Lord." After that he was very careful to avoid parking on our neighbor's property when he came to our house.

Some months later the man's teenage daughter started attending our church. Soon his wife and son came. Not long afterward, the man himself started coming and committed his life to Jesus. He told Peter, "After you wrote that note asking for my forgiveness, my attitude changed. I confronted my own anger and bitterness."

When the man died suddenly a few years later, Pastor Lord conducted the funeral and shared his story. The forgiveness factor made the difference in bringing this family into fellowship with God and with our church.

It's a lesson we all need to learn repeatedly: Admitting our wrongdoing and asking for forgiveness—and freely forgiving those who offend us—is the key to receiving forgiveness ourselves and to seeing our prayers answered.

WILL YOU FORGIVE ME?

My friend Beth shares how she and her husband Floyd handled a problem with forgiving one of their children. They discovered one Saturday that their fourteen-year-old daughter Julee and a neighbor's daughter had gone without permission on a "car date" with a young hippie-type.

Beth and Floyd walked the floor and prayed, asking God to put a hedge of protection around her. Then they bound Satan and all demonic spirits from entrapping Julee.

Later that evening, as Floyd was about to leave for his nightshift job, Julee called. "Mom, can you come get me?" she asked plaintively.

"I'll be there right away," Beth answered.

Before leaving she and Floyd talked over how to handle the matter. They decided if Julee asked their forgiveness, they would give it, but then call a family council to discuss the issue. They then drove both their cars to the address.

Julee was sitting on the curb anxiously waiting for them. "I'll see you at family council tomorrow—I've got to go to work," Floyd told her. He drove off, leaving Beth to cope with a very distraught teenager.

"Mom, I didn't do anything, honest!" Julee cried, falling into her mother's arms.

"You get in the car and wait for me," Beth replied sternly, rushing inside the unfamiliar house. Horrified, she found the house filled with spaced-out teenagers; liquor bottles and burnt-out marijuana joints were everywhere. She found her neighbor's daughter, pulled her outside, and led her to the car.

"Don't say a word to me right now," Beth said, struggling to control her anger as she drove the girls back across town. "I need time to think this through."

Julee cried all the way home. After the other girl had gone home, Julee blurted out, "Mom, will you forgive me?"

"Yes, I will," Beth answered—though she really didn't feel very forgiving at the time.

"Will Daddy forgive me?" Julee asked, still weeping.

"You'll have to ask him. Want to write him a note?"

Julee scrawled on a sheet of notebook paper, "*Daddy, I'm sorry. Will you forgive me? Love, Julee,*" and left it on the dining room table. After he had come home from work and gone to bed, she came out of her room to find his response.

With great relief she read, "*I forgive you. Love, Dad.*"

Meanwhile, Floyd and Beth decided they would deal with the matter by teaching Julee a lesson in unconditional forgiveness.

"WHAT ABOUT YESTERDAY?"

The next day Floyd and Beth and their three girls sat around the table for family council. "Does anyone need to discuss anything this morning?'' Floyd asked. He glanced around the circle. "Beth, do you have anything to bring up?''

"No, I don't," she answered, shaking her head.

"What about yesterday?'' Julee asked anxiously, looking from one parent to the other.

"What about yesterday?'' Floyd asked.

"Daddy, you know!'' Julee exclaimed.

"No, I don't know," he answered, handing her his Bible. "Now, Julee, please read our devotional. I've written out these references for today."

She opened the Bible and read before the entire family:

And when you stand praying, if you hold anything against anyone, forgive him, so that your Father in heaven may forgive you your sins. (Mark 11:25)

And do not grieve the Holy Spirit of God. . . . Get rid of all bitterness, rage and anger, brawling and slander, along with every form of malice. Be kind and compassionate to one another, forgiving each other, just as in Christ God forgave you. (Ephesians 4:30-32)

Then Peter came to Jesus and asked, "Lord, how many times shall I forgive my brother when he sins against me? Up to seven times?'' Jesus answered, "I tell you, not seven times, but seventy-seven times.''

(Matthew 18:21, 22)

Julee was completely disarmed by her parents' act of total forgiveness. As she read the verses of Scripture she and her sisters wept. Floyd closed the meeting with prayer, thanking God for his love and forgiveness. They never again mentioned Julee's disobedience.

AN APOLOGY

One day almost a year later a nice-looking young man knocked on their door and asked to speak with Beth.

"You don't know me, but I'm the one who took your daughter off to a pot party last summer," he explained. I joined the church youth group in order to meet young, innocent kids like Julee and introduce them to drugs. The idea was to get them hooked so they would depend on us for their supply."

Beth invited him to sit down while he told the rest of the story. "Your fourteen-year-old daughter wouldn't try anything at that party," he continued. "She even slapped a Coca-Cola out of my hand. I refused to take her home, and that's when she called you. I was angry that a fourteen-year-old girl had more self-control than I did at eighteen.

"I began searching for meaning in my life after that, and finally found it in Jesus Christ. Now I'm working as an undercover agent, trying to snatch young people out of the drug culture. But I apologize to you for what happened with Julee last summer."

How glad Floyd and Beth were that they had reacted to Julee's disobedience with love and forgiveness! Never again did any of their three daughters go on a date without getting permission.

IT JUST ISN'T FAIR!

Judging by the prayer needs people constantly share with me, unfairness and hurt feelings between Christians are a major problem for many of us. "Divide and conquer" is the tactic the enemy often uses to inhibit the spiritual growth and effectiveness of the Body of Christ.

Aimee's story is typical. She worked for a major Christian ministry, carrying a heavy workload in her understaffed department. When her supervisor resigned she ran the department almost single-handedly, assuming she would be promoted to the supervisor's position and other workers would be hired to help.

After weeks of wondering and waiting, Aimee learned indirectly through someone else that the president of the ministry had hired a young man for the supervisor's position. Angry and hurt, she took a friend to lunch and poured out her frustrations.

"It just isn't fair!" she fumed at Helen. "Lee is young enough to be my son. He knows nothing about this ministry, has precious little experience, and I have to train him to be my supervisor! The fact that no one even had the courtesy to tell me about this personally makes it even worse."

"YOU KNOW YOU HAVE TO FORGIVE"

Helen took a sip of her milkshake, then said quietly, "You know you have to forgive your boss for this, don't you? What he did is wrong and unfair—but that's between him and the Lord. Your response is the important thing, and you can't afford the luxury of bearing a grudge."

"I wish I could just quit and put the whole thing behind me," Aimee said angrily. "Let Lee figure out for himself how to do all that work."

"Well, I'll pray with you about it and ask the Lord to show you what to do," Helen replied. "But you can't quit while you're angry. You have to do it in the right spirit."

Aimee struggled with her anger—and her guilt for feeling angry—for several weeks, asking for the Lord's help to forgive her boss, to forgive Lee, and to do her work with a godly attitude.

"It really was a battle," she told me as she shared the experience. "My pride was involved, and that hurt. It was so tempting to look only at the other person's obvious wrongdoing and justify my own bad attitude. But I knew what Helen had told me was true."

"How did you resolve the matter?" I wanted to know.

"I asked the Lord to turn what seemed to me to be so unfair into something good," Aimee said. "With his help, I was finally able to forgive the people involved and release them from my judgment. I stayed on the job for several months. Then after everything smoothed out and Lee had learned the work, I resigned without any bitterness or broken friendships."

The Lord soon began to open other doors of opportunity for Aimee that never would have been possible had she been tied to that supervisor's job.

"More than a year later, the president of that ministry praised me in a public meeting for my work," she told me, smiling at the memory. "I just thank God he helped me learn the power of forgiveness and the wisdom of trusting him in spite of circumstances. It has made a world of difference in my relationship with the Lord and with other people, and in my prayer life."

FORGIVENESS: A DECISION AND A PROCESS

Julee's parents *decided* to forgive their child and be kind and compassionate to her. Aimee *chose* to forgive her boss instead of harboring bad feelings. But it's important to remember that forgiveness is not only a decision; it is a *process*.

When wronged by someone close to us, we will feel hurt, angry, rejected, and unfairly treated. Usually the hurt comes first because of the rejection. Then we feel angry about the unfairness of the treatment. Then it's easy to judge the person who wronged us, justify our bad attitude, and hold a grudge which, if not dealt with, becomes a root of bitterness. (See Hebrews 12:15.)

We find an irrefutable spiritual law in God's Word:

". . . A man reaps what he sows" (Galatians 6:7).

"Do not judge, or you too will be judged. For in the same way you judge others, you will be judged, and with the measure you use, it will be measured to you" (Matthew 7:1, 2).

We are not responsible for the actions of those who speak against us, but we are responsible for our own attitudes, actions, and *reactions*. Judging another person—even someone who has sinned against us—and holding onto those hurts actually makes us the warden of our own self-made prison.

Forgiving that person releases him or her from our judgment. Then the heavenly Magistrate can judge in the matter from his vantage point.

Once we make the decision to forgive an aggressor, we must continually bring our negative feelings to the cross. When the old feelings and thought patterns surface, it helps to reaffirm that decision in prayer:

Lord, I choose to forgive my husband for hurting me. Please give me your love with which to love him.

Father, bless my husband and help him at the point of his greatest need. Show him how much you love him, and fill any void in his life with a revelation of you so he will not seek a fraudulent love. Thank you for cleansing me from the sin of unforgiveness, in Jesus' name, Amen.

It is difficult to hold a grudge against someone when you're praying for him with a pure motive. In time the negative feelings will subside and disappear if we refuse to keep replaying the grievance. This is the *process* of forgiveness.

Family members, friends, neighbors, coworkers, fellow believers—any or all of these people close to us are likely to offend or disappoint us in some way. But God requires us to forgive if we want to grow in the Lord and see our prayers answered.

Prayer

Father, I confess that I have been bitter, resentful, angry, and hurt at _____ . I choose to forgive, and I release from my judgment all those who have hurt me. I pull out the root of bitterness and all seeds of resentment by forgiving _____ . Lord, strengthen me to walk in constant forgiveness according to your Word, with your love flowing through me. Help me never to keep others in bondage through my selfish decision to refuse them forgiveness.

I ask your blessings and peace to rest upon _____ . Thank you that Jesus paid the price so we can be forgiven and our sins covered by the blood of Jesus. In his name I pray, Amen.

(I recommend my book *How to Forgive Your Children* for biblical references for our need to forgive others.)

NINE

Prayer Means Battle

BE SOBER, BE VIGILANT; because your adversary the devil walks about like a roaring lion, seeking whom he may devour. Resist him, steadfast in the faith, knowing that the same sufferings are experienced by your brother-hood in the world. (1 Peter 5:8, 9, NKJV)

"When I began praying for my rebellious son I ran into a battle," one mother told me. "Through Bible study, prayer, and practical how-to books and tapes, I learned to do spiritual warfare. I *had* to learn it to survive!"

Christians who pray faithfully for their family and friends quickly discover they are engaged in a battle against a formidable enemy. Praying *for* the person is only part of what is needed. Battling *against* opposing forces is also necessary. To win the contest we consistently put forth our own prayer effort to obtain the Lord's help, and bombard the opposition until victory comes.

In the above verses Peter gives us the identity, the character, the method, and the purpose of our enemy:

1. Our enemy is the devil (not another person).
2. He is destructive by nature.
3. His method is to instill fear. (He roars a lot.)
4. His aim is to consume or annihilate his prey. (You and I and our loved ones—in fact, all mankind—are his intended prey.)

The verses also provide instructions for our behavior as we struggle against this adversary. We must:

1. Remain sober—disciplined or self-controlled.
2. Be vigilant—alert and watchful.
3. Be aggressive in resisting him—not only defensively, but offensively.
4. Remain steadfast in the faith—constant, persistent, and unwavering.

WARFARE BRINGS RESULTS

"Devil, take your hands off my children!" I used to shout as I walked the floor morning after morning when my youngsters were in rebellion.

"The Bible says the seed of the righteous *shall be delivered.* My husband and I *are* righteous because of Jesus' shed blood. Our children are our seed and they *will* be delivered. Satan, loose their wills in the name of Jesus. We have a covenant with God Almighty. That covenant stands and you will *not* prevail."

As I walked I quoted Scriptures declaring my "inheritance rights" for my children. I reminded the Lord that I was standing on the promises in his Word. I'd then glorify the Lord with praises and singing, thanking him for the work of the Holy Spirit in each child's life.

I knew God's covenants were for generations, and he is a faithful God. His promises were to me, my children, and my children's children (Isaiah 59:21; Acts 2:38, 39). But my husband and I had to fight for that inheritance, just as Joshua fought to claim the land promised to him and his people. He had to rout the enemy in order to establish his family there.

USING OUR AUTHORITY

Many believers—ministers included—really do not understand spiritual warfare. My friend Hilda's pastor didn't. "I don't think you should teach on spiritual warfare," he told Hilda one day. "Concentrate on Jesus and not on the devil."

"Pastor, I do concentrate on Jesus and his victory," she answered respectfully. "Jesus taught that we have authority over the evil one. Until I began to use Christ's authority in spiritual warfare, I had four children going to hell. I've learned to bind the enemy's work in my family members' lives. Today *all* my children and grandchildren serve the Lord. I've seen the results of spiritual warfare, and I want to help others."

Perhaps you're in a situation similar to Hilda's. You have family members or friends who are not serving the Lord. You are deeply concerned . . . you pray for them . . .

maybe you've tried to witness to them . . . but nothing happens. Like Hilda, you may need to wage spiritual warfare on behalf of these loved ones. This chapter will give you helpful suggestions for doing this.

RECOGNIZE THE ENEMY

As already mentioned, the devil—or Satan—is our adversary. Legions of demonic spirits do his bidding in his aggression against mankind. Paul describes this enemy:

> For our struggle is not against flesh and blood, but against the rulers, against the authorities, against the powers of this dark world and against the spiritual forces of evil in the heavenly realms. (Ephesians 6:12)

Actually, Satan's quarrel is with God. He exalted himself against God, wanting to be equal with the Most High. Because of his insubordination, he was cast out of heaven, along with a host of rebellious angels. (See Isaiah 14:12-14 and 2 Peter 2:4.) Created in the image of God, we are objects of God's love; and consequently, objects of Satan's wrath. He wants to enlist us to join his revolt.

Satan planted the seeds of rebellion in Eden. When he tempted Adam and Eve to sin, the entire human race was contaminated and man's fellowship with God, his Creator, destroyed. But Jesus, the sinless Son of God, sacrificed himself to make atonement for our sins and reconcile us to God. (See Romans 5:12-18.) His action on our behalf defeated Satan's evil plan, and God exalted his

Son—Jesus—to the place Satan had desired. Paul declares the supremacy of Christ's power over the enemy:

> . . . That power is like the working of his mighty strength, which he [God] exerted in Christ when he raised him from the dead and seated him at his right hand in the heavenly realms, far above all rule and authority, power and dominion, and every title that can be given, not only in the present age but also in the one to come. And God placed all things under his feet and appointed him to be head over everything for the church. (Ephesians 1:19-22)

The chief objective of Satan and his evil forces (following his crushing defeat) has been to malign God's character and cause men and women to rebel against their heavenly Father. Keep in mind then that the person for whom you are praying is a target of the enemy, and prone to believe his lies.

UNBELIEVERS BLINDED TO THE LIGHT

Paul explains it this way: "The god of this age has blinded the minds of unbelievers, so that they cannot see the light of the gospel of the glory of Christ . . ." (2 Corinthians 4:4).

Later, he gives instruction which we can use as a prayer for those in rebellion: "[May] . . . God . . . grant them repentance leading them to a knowledge of the truth, and that they will come to their senses and escape from the trap of the devil, who has taken them captive to do his will" (2 Timothy 2:25b, 26).

The person who makes life difficult for us—and the one for whom we should be praying—is a blinded victim of the devil. But he or she is not our enemy, and we should not treat him or her as such. William Gurnall, a perceptive seventeenth-century writer, clarifies the matter:

> Spend your wrath on Satan, who is your chief enemy. Men are only his puppets. They may be won to Christ's side and so become your friends at last. Anselm explains it in the following manner. "When the enemy comes riding up in battle, the valiant soldier is not angry with the horse, but with the horseman. He works to kill the rider so that he may possess the horse for his own use. Thus must we do with the wicked. We are not to bend our wrath against them, but against Satan who rides them and spurs them on. Let us pray fervently, as Christ did on the cross, that the devil will be dismounted and these miserable souls delivered from him."[1]

In Ephesians 6:11, Paul tells us to "put on the full armor of God so that you can take your stand against the devil's schemes."

We need military strategies from God to stand against the schemes—plans of the devil. Ask the Lord for targets for prayer.

When Paul writes that there are "rulers ... authorities ... powers of this dark world . . . spiritual forces of evil in the heavenly realm ..." he's saying there is a hierarchy of evil spirits.

Our role: to *locate, identify, and pull down enemy strongholds* that are coming against those for whom we're praying.

BINDING THE ENEMY

To conduct spiritual warfare against the enemy, we bind the evil spirits which are operating in the situation we are praying about. Jesus taught his followers concerning this:

> "I will give you the keys of the kingdom of heaven; whatever you bind on earth will be bound in heaven, and whatever you loose on earth will be loosed in heaven." (Matthew 16:19)

> "... No one can enter a strong man's house and plunder his goods, unless he first binds the strong man, and then he will plunder his house." (Mark 3:27, NKJV)

To bind evil spirits means to restrain them, to forbid them to continue their destructive activity in the life of the individual. We do this by addressing the spirits directly.

Then, again through the power of the Holy Spirit, our words loose the person from the enemy's bondage. In prayer we ask the Father to send the Holy Spirit to minister according to his or her need. Our prayer is directed to God. Our warfare is directed at the enemy.

Here is an example of how a mother, her husband, and her prayer partners prayed and did warfare for their son Jerry, an alcoholic who had spent time in prison and had attempted suicide:

> Thank you, Lord, that you have given us authority over all the power of the devil by the blood of Jesus Christ,

who defeated Satan at the cross.

By that authority, and in the name of Jesus, we bind the spirits of delusion, depression, addiction, murder, and suicide trying to destroy Jerry's life. We forbid those spirits to operate, and we cancel all assignments of death made against Jerry by any evil power. We declare he belongs to the kingdom of God, not the kingdom of darkness. We loose Jerry from the bondage of the lie of the enemy; he shall live and not die.

Father, please send your Holy Spirit to minister your love and peace to Jerry. Thank you for opening his blinded eyes and for revealing your truth, in Jesus' mighty and powerful name, Amen.

For many months Jerry's parents and their friends prayed like this. A letter from his father expressing love and forgiveness was the beginning of Jerry's turnaround. He eventually stopped drinking, then prayed, "Lord, come back on the throne of my life." Today he is serving the Lord in victory.

WARFARE FOR HUSBANDS

A friend who counsels women whose husbands are unfaithful advises them to use the principle of binding and loosing, as well as praying for their mates. Like this:

I bind the unclean spirits of adultery, perversion, lust, greed, and deception operating in my husband. I bind the spirit of delusion that causes him to justify his sin, the spirits of lewdness and debauchery influencing him through pornography, and the spirit of selfishness causing him to think only of his own desires. In Jesus' name, loose my husband! All spirits of manipulation, control, and seduction operating through his mistress, you are bound in Jesus' name. I speak confusion to all your evil plans.

Lord God, send the Holy Spirit to convict my husband of sin. Reveal yourself to him and show him the truth that Jesus can set him free from this bondage if he will confess and repent. Give him a way of escape out of this situation. Father, send the Holy Spirit to minister to his deepest emotional and spiritual needs.

Lord, please help me to love him with your love, to be an example of godliness, and to speak to him with the law of kindness in my tongue [see Proverbs 31:26]. I thank you in advance for your mighty work of grace in my husband's life, and in my life, bringing healing and reconciliation. In Jesus' name, Amen.

Of course, a husband can use this same strategy in praying for an unfaithful wife. Or a similar prayer can be offered for anyone involved in adultery. In addition to the warfare and intercession, the one praying must forgive the offender and exhibit love toward him.

As the pray-er seeks the Lord daily, the Holy Spirit will give him wisdom to respond appropriately and strategy for further prayer as he ministers to the people concerned. Just as Joshua used a different strategy for each battle he fought, we must realize that each spiritual battle is different.

ENFORCING CHRIST'S VICTORY

"Prayer is not begging God to do something which he is loathe to do. It is not overcoming reluctance in God," writes Paul Billheimer. "It is enforcing Christ's victory over Satan. It is implementing upon earth Heaven's decisions concerning the affairs of men. Calvary legally destroyed Satan, and canceled all of his claims. God placed the enforcement of Calvary's victory in the hands of the church (Matthew 18:18 and Luke 10:17-19). He has given her 'power of attorney.' She is his 'deputy.' But this delegated authority is wholly inoperative apart from the prayers of a believing church. Therefore, prayer is where the action is."[2]

Though the Scriptures boldly declare God's almighty power and Christ's victory over Satan, we often struggle to believe that his Word is really true *for us*. Or that his power and victory will be applied to our situation.

Pastor Billheimer goes on to say, "Unbelief in the integrity of the Word is the first great cause for prayer-lessness."[3] We put our confidence in the reliability of God's Word and choose to believe God is who he says he is, and that he will do what he said he will do.

SCRIPTURE, VISION, DECLARATION, FULFILLMENT

When I began diligently praying for my children, the Lord led me to meditate on this verse: "All your children shall be taught by the Lord, and great shall be the peace of your children" (Isaiah 54:13 NKJV).

Some weeks later, after putting one child on a plane following a Labor Day visit, my heart was heavy. There was no indication of a turning toward the Lord. In church later that day as I closed my eyes in prayer, I suddenly had an inner vision of all three of our children with arms raised, praising the Lord.

I went home and recorded it in my prayer diary. I began to declare with my mouth, "The Lord *is* my children's teacher...their peace shall be great. Thank you, Lord, that you will fulfill your promise, and some day I *will* see them praising you."

Eight months later each child came from a different city to meet me in Orlando for Mother's Day. During worship in church that morning I looked up to see all three of them, hands raised, praising the Lord! What a Mother's Day gift!

I learned what I say with my mouth is important. It is all too easy to talk about the negatives in a situation, when instead I should open my mouth to wield the Sword of the Spirit by quoting the Word of God and declaring what God says in the matter. (See Hebrews 4:12.)

We use our mouths also to declare praises to the Lord for what his shed blood has accomplished and to give testimony to others of his faithfulness. We can just pray, as David did, "May the words of my mouth and the meditation of my heart be pleasing in your sight, O LORD, my Rock and my Redeemer" (Psalm 19:14).

THE POWER OF CHOICE

Neither God nor any person can force another to accept salvation—we cannot overwhelm another's free will. God created men and women with the power of choice, a power that sets us apart from other created beings. However, by waging warfare against the devil and his evil spirits, we can inhibit their activity in a person's life and loose the individual's will so he or she can make a clear decision without interference.

Through prayer and intercession we enlist help from heaven for the individual's salvation and other needs.

Our spiritual battles are fought from a position of victory, since the result of the conflict was assured when Christ completed his work. Our part is to remain zealous in prayer and spiritual warfare to enforce that victory.

FASTING IN WARFARE

Fasting—a voluntary abstinence from food—was a common practice among Jews mentioned numerous times in both the Old and New Testaments. Through the prophet Isaiah, God declares the purpose of fasting: "Is not this the kind of fasting I have chosen: to loose the chains of injustice and untie the cords of the yoke, to set the oppressed free and break every yoke?" (Isaiah 58:6).

"We must not think of fasting as a hunger strike designed to force God's hand and get our own way!" writes Bible teacher Arthur Wallis. "The man who prays with fasting is giving heaven notice that he is truly in earnest; that he will not give up nor let God go without the blessing."[4]

Jesus' temptation in the wilderness, a forty-day period during which he fasted, is the only biblical record of Jesus fasting. But fasting appears important in his overcoming Satan's attack and reinforcing his own spiritual fortitude. He told his followers *"when"* you fast, not *"if"* you fast, indicating he expected them to fast.

He went into the wilderness "full of the Holy Spirit." After the forty-day fast and his victory over Satan's temptations, "Jesus returned to Galilee *in the power of the Spirit . . .*" (Luke 4:1, 14, emphasis added.)

Fasting has several benefits:

1. You can concentrate on prayer and Bible reading. (The effective prayer warrior maintains a close relationship with God through prayer, and reading and meditating on his Word.)

2. You are more sensitive to the spiritual realm, more able to readily respond to the Holy Spirit.

3. The Word of God seems to come alive with deeper meaning during times of fasting, strengthening your faith and making you more bold to assail the enemy.

4. The Holy Spirit often gives strategic revelation as to how to pray or conduct spiritual warfare for the person or situation you are holding before the Lord.

Times of fasting can be wonderfully rewarding spiritually, but trying and difficult physically. Arthur Wallis provides a wise perspective in the matter:

You should expect that a season of fasting would prove to be for you, as it was for your Master, a time of conflict with the powers of darkness. Satan will often try to take advantage of your physical condition to launch an attack. Discouragement is one of his weapons. Guard against it by maintaining a spirit of praise. . . .

Often in seasons of prayer and fasting you will find the going harder instead of easier, and will seem to experience less rather than more liberty. This is often when most is happening. This is wrestling. This is heavenly warfare. Your Captain did not promise you a walk-over but a fight, and gave you the weapons to win . . .

When exercised with a pure heart and a right motive,

fasting may provide us with a key to unlock doors where other keys have failed; a window opening up new horizons in the unseen world; a spiritual weapon of God's providing, "mighty to the pulling down of strongholds." (2 Corinthians 10:4)[5]

Some Christians have a mistaken idea that fasting is only for the "super saints"—those whom they perceive to be spiritually superior. That is a trick of the enemy.

One Texas homemaker told me, "When the Lord called me to a one-week fast to pray for my son, I was sure I wasn't 'spiritual' enough to complete it."

"Did you?" I asked.

"Yes, it was an amazing experience, even though it wasn't easy. The Lord spoke to me daily through my Bible reading, and gave me understanding and strategy for the situation I was praying about. I prepared meals for my family, went to the bedroom to pray while they were eating, then had a good time of fellowship with the Lord while doing dishes."

"Did you eat anything at all?"

"Only water and clear, diluted juices—and the Lord sustained my strength," she replied. "I learned I *could* do it. After that, I fasted every Friday for a year. It made a real difference in improving my relationship with my son."

Fasting should be done with caution, particularly for an individual with health problems. Studying the Bible and reading recommended Christian books on fasting can be helpful. A partial fast—taking only liquids, or eliminating meats and heavy foods—often can be carried out even by those with medical restrictions. It is essential for each individual to follow the leading of the Holy Spirit in determining when, how, and how long to fast.

PRAISE: A MIGHTY WEAPON

If we focus on the trouble Satan is causing in the person or in the resistance of the one for whom we are praying, we soon despair. How important it is that we keep our sights on God and his almighty power, not on the problem, no matter how impossible it appears.

The best way to do this is to enter into praise. We don't need to wait until we see results in the natural to praise the Lord—that requires no faith at all. We declare our faith in God's promise and Christ's victory when we praise him—and we praise him for what he is doing in the supernatural realm, no matter what is happening in the natural realm.

Look at two examples in Scripture where praise was the strategy that defeated the enemy:

> ... Jehoshaphat appointed men to sing to the LORD and to praise him for the splendor of his holiness as they went out at the head of the army, saying: "Give thanks to the LORD, for his love endures forever." As they began to sing and praise, the LORD set ambushes against the men of Ammon and Moab and Mount Seir who were invading Judah, and they were defeated.
>
> (2 Chronicles 20:21, 22)

> After they had been severely flogged, they were thrown into prison, and the jailer was commanded to guard them carefully.... About midnight Paul and Silas were praying and singing hymns to God, and the other prisoners were listening to them. Suddenly there was such a violent earthquake that the foundations of the prison were shaken. At once all the prison doors flew

open, and everybody's chains came loose.

(Acts 16:23, 25, 26)

In the first case, three invading armies were defeated because praises to the Lord set them into confusion and they destroyed one another. In the second account, God's response to the praises Paul and Silas offered in prison was to send an earthquake to liberate them.

In both incidents, the situation seemed without a solution in the natural. Also, in both events, praise was offered *before* deliverance came. Effective Christian warriors eventually learn to praise God despite adverse circumstances. "We live by faith, not by sight," wrote the apostle Paul (2 Corinthians 5:7).

Paul Billheimer points out the personal value of praise:

Here is one of the greatest values of praise: it decentralizes self. The worship and praise of God demands a shift of center from self to God. One cannot praise without relinquishing occupation with self. When praise becomes a way of life, the infinitely lovely God becomes the center of worship rather than the bankrupt self.[6]

GET MOVING TO GAIN CONFIDENCE

The best way to learn spiritual warfare is to do it! Like learning to ride a bicycle, you can't make progress and develop skill until you get moving. But once underway, you learn to stay balanced, you gain confidence, and soon you teach somebody else what you've learned.

Paul Billheimer, a twentieth-century authority on

prayer and author of *Destined for the Throne* said his own salvation resulted from spiritual warfare waged on his behalf. He explains:

> My mother used these weapons on me. I was as hostile to God as any sinner. I was fighting with all my might. But the time came when it was easier to lay down my arms of rebellion than to continue my resistance. The pressure exerted upon me by the Holy Spirit became so powerful that I voluntarily sought relief by yielding my rebellious will. The wooing of divine love was so strong that of my own free will I fell into the arms of redeeming grace. I became a willing "captive."[7]

Doesn't it amaze you what our prayers can accomplish?

A visiting Bible teacher summed it up well:

> *"Our intercession restricts satanic forces and allows the Holy Spirit to bring about conviction, repentance and godly change."*

When we get to heaven and meet all the people we helped get there through our warfare and intercession, we'll see with our eyes what we already know in our heart: the reward is worth the fight!

Prayer

Father, help us fight the good fight of faith.

TEN

Strength in Numbers

AGAIN, I TELL YOU that if two of you on earth agree about anything you ask for, it will be done for you by my Father in heaven. For where two or three come together in my name, there am I with them.

(Matthew 18:19, 20)

"Please pray for my dad to recover quickly from pneumonia," Terry said, stopping me after church. "We're really concerned about him."

"I'll do more than that," I answered. "I'll call our intercessors' prayer chain and ask them to pray, too. I'm a firm believer in two or more agreeing in prayer—there's strength in numbers."

Private prayer is important and necessary, but praying with a prayer partner can strengthen our effectiveness. Jesus never did or said anything except what the Father told him to do—thus he was always in agreement with his heavenly Father. The word *agree* in the above Scripture is derived from a Greek word from which we get our English word "symphony." It means "to be in accord or in harmony" or "to make one mind."

We pray and ask the Lord for his mind about a matter,

then we pray in agreement—or with one mind—with a spouse or prayer partner until we see results.

MY PARTNERS

For years my prayer partner Lib and I prayed over the phone together each weekday morning at 8:00 A.M. for our seven children, our husbands, and one another. Since our youngsters were near the same ages, our husbands employed at the same place, and Lib and I had maintained a similar relationship with the Lord for the same time span, we found it a perfect arrangement for us.

I also had a special friend, Laura, "older in the Lord" than I, who prayed with me twice a month either at her home or mine. Lib, Laura, and I often cried out to God for mercy as we interceded on behalf of our families and learned to trust in his faithfulness.

When I moved to another part of the state I had to find a new prayer support group. But I still keep in close contact with Lib and Laura as we pray for our families—which now include in-law children and grandchildren.

My best partner, however, continues to be my husband, and we pray every day together for our family.

TWO CHRISTIAN MOTHERS

Let me tell you about a prayer partnership between two Christian neighbors whose children attend the same schools.

It was still dark and bitterly cold that December morning—even by northern California standards—as I joined Jane and Katie for their Monday morning prayer meeting. Driving through the dark toward the schools their children attended, I learned that every Monday morning for three years Katie and Jane had been going to the high school and then to the middle school, praying for the teachers, staff, and students.

"Between us we have seven children enrolled in these schools," Jane explained. "We feel it's important to pray for the people who daily influence our youngsters."

"Sometimes we do spiritual warfare and come against the evil forces that pressure and lure children into ungodly situations," Katie told me. "We try to be sensitive and pray as the Holy Spirit directs us."

LISTENING FOR ANSWERS

Sitting in the back seat listening while these two mothers talked to God out loud in very specific detail, I felt engulfed by the presence of the Lord. Their prayers went something like this:

"Lord, you know Laurie's math teacher, Mr. Smith, is very ill."

"We understand his cancer may be terminal."

"Is there something you want us to do for him—besides pray for his healing?"

Silence—complete silence.

Soon Jane spoke up. "Oh, yes, Lord, you want us to volunteer to help in his class. We can do that. And how about Susan's English teacher who has been so out-of-sorts lately? Being short-tempered is not normal behavior for her. Perhaps she has a problem at home. . . . Lord, what can we do for her?"

More silence. Now Katie spoke up.

"You want us to bake her some Christmas cookies and

write her a note of appreciation to encourage her?"

"We'll do that, Lord."

After a half-hour of prayer for teachers and students at the high school, Jane started the car and drove to the nearby middle school. It was still pitch dark and we were the only car in the parking lot.

"Since we began praying three years ago, we understand from staff and students that the drug problem at this middle school is completely gone," Jane informed me.

"Drug problem gone?" I asked, surprised.

"That's what we've been told—but that doesn't mean they don't need prayer in other areas," she added.

For thirty more minutes these mothers prayed for students, faculty, and office staff at the middle school. Then mauve clouds whipped across the sky as daylight dawned and we headed back to their neighborhood.

I learned they meet Wednesday mornings to pray specifically for their own families.

"We've really seen God move in our families since then," Katie reported. "My husband goes to Bible studies with me one night a week, and our children spend a few minutes in prayer and Bible reading in the mornings. I feel it's a result of our prayer."

"Besides that, we encourage one another," Jane added. "We decided two mothers praying in agreement was better than one praying alone."

PRAYER SUPPORT

I thought about Moses' support team—Aaron and Hur—as an example of strength in numbers. Israel's leader was standing on a hill overlooking the valley where his troops were fighting an invading army.

As long as Moses held up his hands and held out his staff over the valley, Israel was winning. But as weariness caused his hands to droop, the enemy would get the upper hand. Aaron and Hur stood on either side of Moses and held up his hands until sunset; thus Israel won the victory. (See Exodus 17:8-13.)

I praised the Lord for my own support team back in Destin, Florida—Fran, Ginger, Claire, Patsy, and Susan. We meet together early one morning a week to pray for our families.

But what really excited me was that Jane and Katie cared enough to go to the schools and pray for those in authority over their children—the teachers.

A CONGREGATION PRAYS

Critical situations often arise on the mission field, which means those serving on the front lines need special prayer support from intercessors back home.

During an attempted coup in a Caribbean country last year an orphanage ministry faced the crisis of running out of food and drinking water. Stores were closed and any vehicles venturing onto the streets were in danger of being attacked by rebels.

The ministry leader was out of the country and two young women were in charge. The adults skipped meals so the fifty-five children could eat. Then the water purifier broke down and they had to melt purified ice cubes from the freezer for the babies' drinking water. The last bit of food was almost gone.

One of the missionaries finally got a message through to a pastor in Texas who changed the order of worship that Sunday morning—at the prompting of the Holy Spirit—and called his entire congregation to pray together specifically for three things: for food and water to be provided, for the young missionaries in charge to have wisdom in making decisions, and that fear would not overwhelm those on the compound.

Within the hour all those prayers were answered. The missionaries decided to send the driver out to search for food, even though markets normally don't open on Sunday. He felt led to go the opposite direction from his usual shopping route, though that meant driving away from the city.

He found a village open market stocked with plenty of fresh vegetables, and he located enough bottled water to last until the purifier could be repaired.

When he returned with provisions, the children and workers were already singing and dancing—all fear was gone. They gave God thanks for the food with rejoicing and enjoyed the best meal they'd had for days. Meanwhile, the Texas congregation felt gratified and thrilled that the Holy Spirit had used them.

TWO DAUGHTERS IN AGREEMENT

Sometimes children stand in the prayer gap for parents. Meg came from Ohio and Gina from Florida for their parents' anniversary in Kentucky. During the visit they were horrified as they observed the screaming and arguing between Mom and Dad—who had reared their six children in a Christian home.

"What has happened? What can we do?" the girls asked one another.

"As far away as we are from them and from each other, we can't do anything but pray," Gina concluded.

"Yes, we can agree in prayer," Meg offered.

Every Friday morning at eight o'clock they prayed:

Lord, what we want is for you to become top priority in our parents' lives. Come as their Peacemaker. Draw Mom and Dad back to you, in Jesus' name, Amen.

After a year of praying, they learned their mother had colon cancer. She was fearful, but finally agreed to radiation treatments.

One day Gina phoned her sister. "I know God did not give her cancer, but maybe he will turn this illness for good in Mom's life. Let's pray that way. And also that he will heal her."

"I agree," her sister echoed.

They kept praying and God moved. Meg got a phone call one night from her mom.

"I want you to know I've come to depend on God through this cancer ordeal," she told her daughter. "I haven't done that in ages. I've also found out what a wonderful help your dad can be. We want you to come home again soon."

When I visited Meg in Ohio recently she told me, "Mom has been free of cancer for six years now. And peace and harmony between Mom and Dad is evident in their home."

The prayer of agreement is a spiritual dynamic which cannot be explained by logic. I pray in agreement with other intercessors all the time, and I hear testimonies of its effectiveness everywhere I go.

A MOTHER AND HER PRAYER PARTNER

In response to her father's unrelenting verbal abuse, nine-year-old Alice slipped into a state of depression one November afternoon. She stopped playing, laughing, and chatting with her friends on the phone. Gathering up her dolls, she gave them all away.

"I knew I couldn't undo the emotional damage just by trying to talk her out of the gloomy mood," her mother, Joyce, told me. "So I called my prayer partner, and we prayed in agreement for Alice, binding the spirit of depression that seemed to engulf her. Then in whatever ways I could I tried to compensate for my husband's attitude by showing her love and acceptance."

Joyce prayed Scripture for her daughter over the next weeks and months, in agreement with her prayer partner.

Then our sons in their youth will be like well-nurtured plants, and our daughters will be like pillars carved to adorn a palace. . . .There will be no breaching of walls, no going into captivity, no cry of distress in our streets.
(Psalm 144:12, 14)

She paraphrased Isaiah 54:17:

No weapon formed against my daughter shall prosper; the tongue raised against her is refuted. Lord, come and show yourself mighty on her behalf.

On a warm spring evening six months later, Alice accepted her mom's offer to take her and her best friend to play in the park. That alone was a victory! At the playground they ran barefoot in the grass and took turns pushing each other on an old tire swing.

Joyce watched as Alice pushed her friend on the swing, fell into the sandpile laughing hilariously, then took her turn swinging. She went home covered with so much sand that Joyce had to hose her down before bathing her that night. Not only did her depression lift, but Alice's relationship with her father began to improve.

"I had my daughter back!" Joyce told me, jubilant. "I gave her the dolls I had as a little girl and she's playing with them—loving them as I used to do."

NEBRASKA PRAY-ERS

Only thirty-seven students were scheduled to graduate from the tiny, rural Nebraska school, but some concerned parents decided that year they didn't want any wild drinking parties or car accidents.

Sheila, a Christian mother of one graduate, opened her home for prayer. Nightly for three weeks before the end of the school term, any parent of a graduating senior was invited to come for prayer. Usually at least four came, and they always prayed together in agreement following this pattern:

1. They prayed for each student by name, asking God to bless him or her as he or she graduated, sought a job, or went off to college.
2. They prayed there would be no deaths or serious accidents resulting from drinking and driving.
3. They prayed against the confusion often accom-

panying the awards part of the commencement service—whistling, screaming, or yelling during the ceremonies. This year they wanted none of that disrespect.

What happened?
All these prayers were answered.
No incidents either at commencement exercises or in the celebration afterward marred this special time for the young people and their families. Convinced of the power of praying in agreement, these parents planned another prayer session for the next year's graduates.

PRAYER WALK

My friend Sharon, her two daughters, and her daughter-in-law experienced an unusual bonding one year when they decided to take a "prayer walk" together around their husbands' farmlands.

When spring planting began, the women started their walks. They prayed in the fields where their husbands would be planting wheat, and later corn, grain, and soy beans.

Going from fence post to fence post, most days they walked two miles but on some days they covered six miles.

They prayed specifically for protection over the land, asking God to keep it free from insect damage, crop disease, hail, and drought. They prayed individually for their four husbands, asking God to give them wisdom about planting, selling, and marketing. They also asked the Lord to dispatch angels to watch over them and their farm helpers as they worked the fields.

As they walked, they prayed for their neighbors' fields which touched their own, asking the Lord to bless and protect their crops as well.

"We saw amazing results," Sharon told me. "It was one of our better years. Some farmers felt the bankruptcy pressure really hard that year. Others made unwise marketing decisions when their yields were down and their margin was just too slim. But our husbands made prudent decisions. Our crops made a profit, and we had no storm or insect damage. Best of all, our family was knit closer as we women prayed for our husbands and our farms—our very livelihood.

"Did your husbands think you were a little fanatic?" I asked, smiling.

"Actually, our men liked the idea," Sharon responded. "They helped us to know which boundary lines to walk as we prayed. And one husband agreed for his wife to hire a babysitter so she could participate.

"Looking back, I sometimes wonder why we don't do it every year. Perhaps it was a special season of our lives. But we definitely did see results."

EARLY MORNING PRAYER GROUP

The other night Emily called from two hundred miles away to share an exciting report.

"I heard you at the fall retreat," she said, reminding me where we'd met. "At first I rebelled at the idea of meeting early in the morning to pray in agreement. But on the way home the Lord convinced me to open my house on Monday mornings and invite any Christian woman who wanted to come."

Emily told me she set some specific rules: Her house is open from five to six o'clock every Monday morning for prayer; no coffee or conversation is permitted before prayer.

"We've seen fantastic results in the six months since we've been praying together," she reported excitedly. "Two children have been saved . . . one son found a wonderful Christian mate . . . one husband received the baptism of the Holy Spirit. We have from four to eight women every Monday.

"My husband stays in the back of the house until time for his breakfast—and that's when all the praying women leave."

Over the years I've been in several prayer support groups. There are all kinds of ways to organize one, but here are some guidelines that worked well for us:

1. Keep the group small (two to six—not more than ten).
2. Pray. Don't gossip.
3. Protect confidentiality shared in the group.
4. Meet and adjourn on time. Decide in advance a regular time and place to meet, such as every Monday night from 7:00 to 8:00 P.M. at the Smith's, or Wednesdays from 10:00 to 11:30 A.M. at Suzy's, or on lunch break at your workplace once or twice a week.
5. If it is a group of only two or three, it should be either all women or all men; a larger group of men and women praying together is fine. An individual prayer partner, other than your spouse, should always be your same sex.

Whatever prayer team combination works for you in the current season of your life, do it. If you don't have a prayer partner, ask God for one and discipline yourself to pray in agreement together on a regular basis.

Prayer

Father, show me who you want me to pray with on a regular basis. Bring the name of that person to my mind and move on his heart also if it is your plan for us to become a prayer team.

Lord, please show me which prayer support system I'm to be attached to. Bring me into fellowship with a group of Christians willing to help carry my prayer burden. Help me also to be an encouragement to them. Thank you, Lord, for these special people you will bring across my path. Amen.

ELEVEN

Praying with Persistence

THEN JESUS TOLD HIS DISCIPLES A PARABLE to show them that they should always pray and not give up. (Luke 18:1)

Lying on the floor of a filthy prison, chained to two soldiers, Peter must have felt that his situation was hopeless. Guarded by four squads of soldiers (sixteen armed men), he finally fell asleep.

Only days before, King Herod had arrested James and ordered him put to death by the sword. When this action earned Herod favor with the Jews, he then seized Peter and locked him up until after the Passover. Clearly, Peter was slated to be the next martyr of the church.

Herod, however, wasn't counting on the power of persistent prayer. While Peter slept, the believers gathered at John Mark's mother's home and were "earnestly praying to God for him" (Acts 12:5). The word *earnestly*, which comes from a root verb meaning "to stretch," implies the idea of not relaxing in effort.

Suddenly an angel of the Lord appeared in the prison cell, awakened Peter, and gave him orders to get dressed and follow. Chains fell off Peter's hands; he grabbed his cloak and sandals and followed the angel past all the guards and out of the prison. When they came to the iron gate leading to the city, it opened by itself. The angel stayed with the apostle for a while, then disappeared. Peter made his way to his friends' house where the prayer meeting was still going on.

Isn't it amazing that these Christian friends, who were still engaged in fervent prayer for his release, had a hard time believing Peter was actually standing there knocking on the gate, free from prison? They probably looked at one another with astonishment and said, "It worked! Our prayers really worked!"

This story in Acts 12 encourages us to believe for amazing results in response to persistent prayer, even when the faith of the pray-ers is less than perfect!

"MY BOY'S GOING TO MAKE IT"

Ellen was a mother and widow who persistently prayed for her five children after she was left to rear them alone. When gathering them around their father's casket, she had prayed, "Lord, I don't have anything to give you except myself and these children, but we commit ourselves to you and trust you to take care of us."

Hardships hit, but with her faith in God steadfast, she continually declared, "We're going to make it!" When the state welfare agent wanted to place one boy, Charles, in an orphanage to lighten her load, she refused. "We may not look like much, but we're going to make it," she announced stubbornly to the agent who came to the farm to get Charles.

Years passed. The children stayed true to the Lord, and most of them entered the ministry—all except one. When the middle boy, Melvin, joined the army, he fell into the ways of the world, married an unbeliever, and forsook the faith of his childhood; Ellen never stopped praying for her wayward son. Every time friends or family members lamented over Melvin's spiritual condition, she had a standard response: "God doesn't lie—I'll never stop believing. My boy's going to make it!"

One day Charles received word that his unsaved brother Melvin had died suddenly of a heart attack. He immediately flew to Boston and went directly to the funeral home. As he stood before his brother's casket wondering how his mother would respond to the shocking news, Melvin's wife came into the room.

"Charles, I want to tell you something that happened last night that I think will make you feel better," she said. "I had gone to bed ahead of Melvin. A little later he went from room to room to tell all the children goodnight, then came to our bedroom. But instead of getting into bed he did something I've never seen him do in all the years we've been married. He knelt beside the bed and began praying. Then I noticed he was praying in a strange language—a language I've never heard him speak before. After a little while he got into bed and went to sleep. Early this morning he had the heart attack and died."

His fears relieved, Charles phoned his mother's home and recounted the story. "Well, Mom, what do you think?" he asked.

Strong and confident her voice came back, so real he could almost see her Irish eyes sparkling. "I think my boy made it!" Ellen said triumphantly.

PERSISTENT AND SPECIFIC PRAYER

When the disciples asked Jesus to teach them to pray, he taught them what we've come to call the Lord's Prayer, but then he immediately told them a parable which illustrates persistent prayer.

A neighbor knocks on a friend's door at midnight asking for three loaves of bread for his unexpected guests. The friend shouts, "Don't bother me. The door is already locked, and my children are with me in bed. I can't get up and give you anything" (Luke 11:7).

But the neighbor keeps on knocking. Because of his boldness, his friend finally gets up and gives him as much as he wants. Jesus added, "So I say to you: Ask and it will be given to you; seek and you will find; knock and the door will be opened to you. For everyone who asks receives; he who seeks finds; and to him who knocks, the door will be opened" (Luke 11:9, 10).

In other words, Jesus is teaching us to be *persistent, bold,* and *specific* in asking him to answer our prayers. Bible teacher Jack Hayford says of this parable:

It is mind-boggling to understand why this passage has been used to show that prayer must earn answers through overcoming God's reluctance, as if our persistence could overcome God's resistance.

In fact, Jesus is saying, "Your first barrier isn't God—

it's your own hesitance to ask freely. You need to learn the kind of boldness that isn't afraid to ask—whatever the need or the circumstance."

The lesson revolves around one idea: shameless boldness. . . . Boldness is your privilege. Your assignment is to ask; his commitment is to give—as much as you need.

This is the beginning. "Seeking" and "knocking" are further steps. . . . Too many hesitate to pray. They hesitate through a sense of unworthiness, a feeling of distance from deity, a wondering about God's will in the matter . . . a fear that God won't hear.

Jesus strikes the death blow to such hesitancy: ask. Ask with unabashed forwardness; ask with shameless boldness, he commands. And when you do, he clearly teaches, "your friend, my Father, will rise to the occasion and see that everything you need is provided."[1]

BE DEFINITE

The man in the parable in Luke chapter eleven is an excellent example for us. He was very *definite* about what he needed—*three loaves of bread*. He could have simply asked for *some bread,* but he wanted three loaves—the exact amount he needed for his unexpected guests' stay.

Also, the midnight hour was not the most opportune time to go banging on the door with such a request, but the man expected his neighbor to rise to the occasion and meet his need. Jesus urges us to ask at any time, no matter what the need or circumstances, and to be bold and specific. (See Luke 11:5-10.)

CRY OUT NIGHT AND DAY

Jesus told his disciples another parable to show them how to pray with persistence. It's the story of a judge who didn't fear God or care about man. When a widow came and begged him to grant her justice against her adversary, at first the judge refused. But finally he reasoned to himself, "Even though I don't fear God or care about men, yet because this widow keeps bothering me, I will see that she gets justice, so that she won't eventually wear me out with her coming!"

Then Jesus told his disciples, "Listen to what the unjust judge says. And will not God bring about justice for his chosen ones, who cry out to him day and night? Will he keep putting them off? I tell you, he will see that they get justice, and quickly." (See Luke 18:1-8 for this story.)

The parable did not mean that God is like the unjust judge. He is not. Rather, the unjust judge is a picture of the evil one. But even he knew from the tone of the widow's voice and her audacious attitude that she would wear him out if she kept coming. Jesus said God will avenge his own elect who cry to him day and night. In a sense he is saying, "Demand your rights from the evil one," and in the same breath assuring us, "I will see that you get justice." Dr. Charles Stanley says,

We must pray until we see an answer—with persistent confidence in the faithfulness of God. . . . Praying with authority is . . . claiming that which has already been bought and paid for by Christ at Calvary. When we pray with the authority God gave us, we will see our prayers become the effective tools they were meant to be.[2]

TRAVAILING PRAYER

Persistent prayer may lead to travailing prayer for a season as we intercede for our loved ones. We see travail in the prayers of Jesus: "During the days of Jesus' life on earth, he offered up prayers and petitions with loud cries and tears . . ." (Hebrews 5:7).

When he saw Mary weeping over her dead brother Lazarus, he "groaned in the spirit and was troubled"; as he approached the tomb to call Lazarus forth he was "groaning in himself" (John 11:33, 38, NKJV). But the travail was followed by victory. Lazarus was raised from the dead!

As we intercede for those who are dead in transgressions and sins, we may groan or offer up loud cries and tears. But through such intercession we can see them become alive in Christ. (See Ephesians 2:1-9.) In the spirit realm, we can call them forth from the tomb.

Evangelist John Dawson makes an important point:

When you truly love somebody, you don't just mention the person before the Lord. You pray *until* that which is needed happens, until the answer comes, until breakthrough. Love settles for nothing less than victory. Love fills us with an earnest ambition for the desired result.

If you are praying for a family member who is in bondage, you are not released from the burden until that person is saved, set free and in order.[3]

The breakthrough you are praying for may take place in the spiritual realm weeks or months before you actually see a change in the situation. You may experience a release in your spirit when that happens and you then move from travail to praise. God's promise is, "Those who sow in tears will reap with songs of joy" (Psalm 126:5).

Maybe this example will better explain. One mom travailed in prayer for some time about her drug addicted daughter. One evening while lying on her face in prayer, she heard the Lord's quiet voice promising that she'd soon be set free. Wiping her tears, that mom got up and began praising God. She'd had a release in her spirit. Time for travail was over. She continued praising God for victory, though there was no outward change in her daughter. Five long months passed. Then when her daughter overdosed, she was ready for help. After some Christian counseling, she was set free.

FIFTY THOUSAND PRAYERS

George Müller was known throughout England in the nineteenth century for providing for thousands of orphans simply by asking God to supply their needs. He estimated that God had answered more than fifty thousand of his prayers, usually on the very day he asked.

But the answers to a few of his prayers—for the salvation of some people he deeply cared for—were delayed. He once wrote:

In November, 1844, I began to pray for the conversion of five individuals. I prayed every day without a single intermission. . . . Eighteen months elapsed before the first of the five was converted. I thanked God and prayed on for the others. Five years elapsed and then the second was converted. . . . Six years passed before the third was converted.

The man to whom God in the riches of his grace has given tens of thousands of answers to prayer in the self-same hour or day in which they were offered has been praying day by day for nearly thirty-six years for the conversion of these (two) individuals, and yet, they remain unconverted. But I hope in God, I pray on, and look yet for the answer. They are not converted yet, but they will be.[4]

For *fifty-two* unfailing years Müller prayed for these two men, sons of a childhood friend of his, without seeing tangible evidence of an answer. When Müller died, the two men were still unconverted. Soon after his death in 1898, however, each of them received Jesus as his Lord.

A few months before he died, Müller had told a friend, "When once I am persuaded that a thing is right and for the glory of God, I go on praying for it until the answer comes. George Müller never gives up!"[5]

Could you and I pray for fifty-two years and know without a shadow of doubt that the answer was on the way? The Lord wants us to exhibit that kind of persistent faith. When we pray for a person's salvation we know that he is free to either accept or reject God, but we also know it is God's will to save him. So we know we are in agreement with his will. Our part is to stand in the gap, in faith, never wavering. George Müller's prayer example is a lesson in faithful persistence and specific asking.

PRAYING SPECIFICALLY

Let's talk more about praying specifically.

When my friend Caroline's son David was a teenager he played such ear-splitting rock music on his guitar that she made him and his band members practice in the storeroom behind her house. The family couldn't stand the noise. Caroline's constant prayer was, "Lord, use that guitar to your service, to make melody for you."

It was a definite prayer, one she prayed often. Did it bring results? Yes, but not exactly the way Caroline had in mind.

While David was in college, he was in an auto accident that crippled his arm. Unable to play, he passed his guitar to his fourteen-year-old brother, Mark. Within a year Mark was playing well enough to accompany his church youth group during their praise and worship sessions. Most of his spare time at home was spent practicing Christian music.

Telling me about it, Caroline said, "The other day I realized how off-base I'd been in praying for the guitar to be used for the Lord. How I wish I had prayed more specifically for David to have a desire to know Jesus and then play the instrument to his glory. Can you believe I prayed for a guitar? Now I'm praying for David to make an all-out commitment to Jesus."

When we pray for definite things, we should expect the Lord to respond, though he may do it in surprising ways!

BED, BICYCLE, BOOTS, BUS TICKETS

As our daughter Sherry was packing to move to Copenhagen with Kim, her Danish husband, we asked one night in a family prayer session how we should pray for her. She gave us a list of immediate needs: *a bed, bicycles, boots, and bus tickets.*

"Wow, Sherry, that's really specific," her sister Quinett said as we sat on the floor in a circle to pray.

They had already rented a fifth floor walk-up apartment that was unfurnished, so they needed a bed first of all. They wouldn't have a car, so they needed money for bus tickets and bicycles. Boots were a must for a Florida girl unaccustomed to cold Scandinavian winters. Within a few weeks after their arrival in Denmark, God provided all these things, so our prayer list changed. Then we began to pray for doors of ministry to open to them, and for Sherry to learn Danish quickly without difficulty.

MONEY, MINISTRY, MATES

During a visit to the Bible school my children attend I was eating lunch in the school cafeteria with my son and three of his close friends, all in their late twenties. They were sharing their needs and future goals with me.

"Hey, guys, it seems I need to pray three M's for you— money, ministry, and mates," I said.

"Right on!" they all agreed. Each of them needed money to finish his schooling; each wanted a specific door of ministry to open when he graduated; and each wanted God's perfect wife for him.

"Mom, don't leave me out of those prayers," my son Keith piped up.

We all laughed. But there amidst the cafeteria noise, we prayed specifically for money, ministry, and mates for each young man.

When Jesus gave us the Lord's Prayer as a guideline for

how to pray, he taught us to pray specifically, "Give us this day our daily bread." We are then to be specific in our prayer requests, and steadfast to pray until they are answered.

May we, like the old prayer warrior Müller declare, "Once I am persuaded that a thing is right and for the glory of God, I will go on praying boldly and specifically until the answer comes!"

Prayer

Lord, I thank you that you have taught us to pray specifically and with persistence, assuring us that when we ask, you hear. When we knock, you open. Thank you for being such a loving, caring Father. Help me to be tenacious and faithful in prayer, I ask in Jesus' name, Amen.

EXERCISE

Ask God to guide you as you list specific things to pray for. Begin to pray for them on a regular basis. From time to time ask the Lord to show you if there is something on the list that needs to be changed or deleted. Search your heart about your motive for these prayer items; be sure it is with a pure heart that you are presenting your specific petitions boldly to the throne of grace. Use this method in praying for loved ones, housing problems, employment, school situations, problems at work, or whatever your need or your loved ones' needs might be.

TWELVE

Overcoming Obstacles

"... DON'T BE AFRAID... Remember the Lord, who is great and awesome, and fight for your brothers, your sons and your daughters, your wives and your homes."

(Nehemiah 4:14)

Fear—Discouragement—Distraction. All these are well-worn tactics the enemy uses against us as we stand in the prayer gap for our family and friends.

Nehemiah and his band of Jewish refugees who set out to rebuild the broken down walls of Jerusalem met these tactics head-on. They were opposed by foes who tried to frighten them, discourage them, and make them quit, or get them distracted enough to stop the work for a season.

WALLS BROKEN DOWN

Some of our family "walls" are broken down because the enemy has been given access to come in through disobedience, rebellion, or neglect on the part of one or more family members, or through jealousy, immorality, idolatry, pride, selfishness, or substance addiction.

Nehemiah, an exiled Jew in Babylon, was cupbearer to the king of Persia when he learned the walls of Jerusalem, home of his ancestors, lay in ruins. He wept, mourned, fasted, and prayed because of the condition of his homeland (a good example for any intercessor). First, he confessed the sins of his forefathers:

> ". . . I confess the sins we Israelites, including myself and my father's house, have committed against you. We have acted very wickedly toward you. We have not obeyed the commands, decrees and laws you gave your servant Moses." (Nehemiah 1:6, 7)

See how he identified with the sin of his family? Confessing the iniquities of our ancestors and family members is an effective way to begin intercession for them:

> Father God, have mercy on us. Forgive us for the sin of _____ that's been in our family for generations. Thank you, Lord, that Jesus came to set us free from the curse of the sins of the forefathers. I pray that each member of my family will receive the cleansing of the blood of Jesus and the deliverance he alone can give. It is in his name that I pray, Amen.

REMIND GOD OF HIS PROMISES

This is the promise God had made to his people:

> ". . . If you return to me and obey my commands, then even if your exiled people are at the farthest horizon, I

will gather them from there and bring them to the place
I have chosen as a dwelling for my Name."

(Nehemiah 1:9)

Nehemiah reminded God that the people now living in
Jerusalem were his people, brought back from exile, and
the walls needed rebuilding to stop their enemies from
having free access to their homes. He asked for favor with
the king so that he could go to Jerusalem and start the
project.

After praying for several months, Nehemiah got the
king's permission to go to Jerusalem to rebuild the walls.
First he scouted out the land at night. Then, calling the
elders together, he shared his plan and they pledged their
cooperation.

After we have "scouted out" the spiritual problems in
our families, we may want to gather a few family members
to join us in prayer to "rebuild the wall." Whenever there
is a breach in the wall, intercessors must work (pray) until
it is closed and the family member(s) rescued or restored.

Nehemiah's prayers are good models for us:

"O Lord, let your ear be attentive to the prayer of this
your servant . . . Give your servant success today . . ."

(Nehemiah 1:11)

"Now, strengthen my hands. . . ." (Nehemiah 6:9)

DEALING WITH THE ENEMY

Nehemiah's foe was Sanballat, who with his com-
panions freely moved in and out of the city since the walls
were in disrepair. He taunted Nehemiah and the Israelites

Israelites, mocking and ridiculing them. He even accused them of rebellion against the king. Nehemiah's answer is one we can use when the enemy taunts us:

". . . The God of heaven will give us success. We his servants will start rebuilding, but as for you, you have no share in Jerusalem or any claim or historic right to it." (Nehemiah 2:20)

Nehemiah talked back to the enemy. In like manner, we must declare to the enemy that we are taking back the territory he has claimed in our family. He has no legal or historic right to it.

This spiritual leader also asked God to cause the enemy's plan against him and his countrymen to backfire. Using his prayer as an example (see Nehemiah 4:4, 5), we can ask God to let the devil's plan of attack against our family turn and bring damage to his own camp. We can also remind Satan that his tactic against Jesus resulted in his own defeat.

Nehemiah posted a guard day and night to meet the enemy's threats. He organized the people so that half of them worked on the wall with their swords at their sides while the other half stood guard with additional weapons.

The enemy continued to taunt God's people, instilling fear and even trying to lure Nehemiah to stop the work and reason with him. But family members worked together until the wall was rebuilt without a gap left in it.

CHOOSING TO BELIEVE GOD'S PROMISE

My Jewish friend Rachel accepted Jesus Christ as her Messiah in a dramatic salvation experience. Though her husband Irving heard the same Bible discussion she did, he refused to respond to the Lord.

While Irving did not openly oppose her decision, he wanted no part of serving the Lord with her. However, God had given Rachel a firm promise: *You will be saved, and your household.* (Based on Acts 16:31.)

At first she tried to bring the promise to reality by persuasion. She did everything she could think of to convince Irving of his need for Jesus. And all the while the enemy was taunting her. "He'll never change. He'll never accept Jesus. You're making a fool of yourself."

Rachel refused to listen to the enemy, choosing to believe God's promise. She prayed, "Lord, I release my husband. I believe you told me our whole house would be saved, but my center is in you, Lord—not Irving's salvation. I'm just going to love him like he is."

It wasn't easy to do. But five years later, after undergoing great financial difficulty and almost losing his professional career, Irving cried out for Jesus to save him. The breach in the wall was closed, their Christian household established.

When Rachel began praying for her husband she never dreamed it would take so long or that they would suffer such great financial loss before he finally yielded to God. The cost was great and the waiting difficult, but the end result made it all worthwhile, she said.

THE JOY OF THE LORD

Nehemiah and the people of Jerusalem had a grand celebration when the work was completed. They listened to the reading of the Word of God. They wept, sang, bowed down, and celebrated as their leader reminded

them, ". . . The joy of the LORD is your strength"
(Nehemiah 8:10).

How true. The joy of the Lord *is* our strength whenever
we become weary or fearful in the battle for our loved
ones. The devil doesn't easily give up his mocking and
accusations, even when it appears the answer has come.

HANDLING DISTRACTIONS

The enemy sees to it that we are distracted during our
daily prayer time, but we frustrate his plan by putting
aside those distractions and getting on with our prayer. I
keep notepaper with my Bible, so when distractions
invade my thoughts I quickly jot them down, and go on
with prayer and praise.

My list might read:

Write Traci
Call Martha re: Friday night
Make plane reservations to New York
Buy vitamins

We need to make up our minds ahead of time what we
will do about other distractions, such as phone calls and
unexpected visitors. I decided to have my time alone with
God very early in the mornings before the phone begins
to ring. Some pastors and businessmen have their secre-
taries hold their calls while they have time with the Lord.
We must give our prayer time priority or the enemy will
steal it.

DEFEATING DISCOURAGEMENT

When discouraged about my prayers not being answered—indeed if things look even worse rather than better—I need a plan against discouragement. My method is to look through my prayer diary and review some of the answers to prayer I've already received. Then I praise the Lord for his faithfulness:

"Lord, I remember how many years it looked absolutely hopeless for my brother-in-law, but he accepted Jesus just weeks before he died. I thank you that *nothing* is impossible with you!"

"I remember how you used one of my children's friends to bring my youngest child back to you. So, Lord, I trust you in this predicament, also."

Besides reviewing the record of answered prayers, I also meditate on the Book of Hebrews. Such verses as these are antidotes to discouragement:

Let us then approach the throne of grace with confidence, so that we may receive mercy and find grace to help us in our time of need. (Hebrews 4:16)

Let us hold unswervingly to the hope we profess, for he who promised is faithful. (Hebrews 10:23)

Jesus Christ is the same yesterday and today and forever. (Hebrews 13:8)

After years of yelling so often, "Help, Lord, help," I now find myself more often whispering, "I do trust you, Lord. Yes, I trust you."

DON'T GIVE IN TO "WHAT IFS"

Fear is a bugaboo that grips many of us. It often starts with "what if?"

"What if my husband goes to hell?"

"What if my dad never stops gambling?"

"What if my child blows his mind with his drug abuse?"

"What if my son goes to prison? I couldn't stand it."

I know several women whose sons are in prison. One told me her son received Jesus as Lord while on death row. With joy over his spiritual transformation, she said, "He's just going to preach his way to heaven."

Another mother is intercessor for her state prison system, grateful that her son too responded to the Savior while behind bars.

Both moms had prayed that their sons would come to know Jesus—and thus have eternal life—and both prayers were miraculously answered. They acknowledge that the young men should pay for their crimes. But where their sons live did not make these Christian women bitter or disheartened. Instead, they committed their sons to God—for his plan and purpose for their lives, even in prison.

WHEN FEAR WORKS OVERTIME

When fear works overtime, how do we handle it? That's a big challenge!

For starters, God says he has not given us a spirit of fear but of a sound mind. So we acknowledge that fear is from the enemy.

Next we choose to "demolish arguments . . . and take captive every thought to make it obedient to Christ." How? By thinking on things that are "true, noble, right, pure, lovely, admirable, excellent or praiseworthy" (2 Corinthians 10:5; Philippians 4:8).

If we pray with holy motives, we must *believe* that God will answer us in his best way. The apostle James admonished us:

> "But when he asks, he must *believe and not doubt*, because he who doubts is like a wave of the sea, blown and tossed by the wind. That man should not think he will receive anything from the Lord."
>
> (James 1:6, 7, italics mine)

I've discovered that if I allow fear to crowd my thoughts for very long, I'm soon into doubt, convinced that what I'm praying for my friend or family member will never come to pass. Fear and doubt then are twin stumbling blocks to answered prayer that I can't afford to have around.

BIND FEAR AND DESPAIR

I was finishing this chapter very late at night when I got an emergency long-distance call.

"I just found a suicide note my twelve-year-old daughter wrote two days ago," my friend said with a distraught voice. "Please pray and fight the devil with me—I'm desperate. There's a pattern of suicide in my husband's family."

I prayed over the phone with her immediately, binding

the spirits of suicide, murder, fear, and destruction. Then I agreed with her that God's peace would permeate their household. By the time our prayer was finished, her fear and despair were replaced by confidence that God was at work.

FIGHT FOR THE FAMILY

Nehemiah's message still speaks to us today—". . . Fight for your brothers, your sons and your daughters, your wives and your homes" (Nehemiah 4:14).

We who live in the so-called "space age" may not easily identify with Nehemiah's wall repair, Joshua's battles, or Noah's ark building. But we are still beset by the same old enemy each of them faced. We have a recourse—the same one they had. Prayer.

We must never see prayer as a "religious form," but as a child speaking with his Father, in the name of Jesus, through the Holy Spirit.

Whether it is discouragement, distraction, or fear, we overcome those obstacles by sticking to the business of prayer, trusting God to bring in our loved ones. He's bigger than any problem or situation looming before us.

Let's continue to stand as unyielding intercessors for our family and friends—rebuilding broken, burned walls that have given the enemy access. For the gracious hand of our God is upon us!

AFFIRMATION

"The God of heaven will give us success. We his servants will start rebuilding . . ." (Nehemiah 2:20a).

Epilogue

MY PART IN COMPLETING THIS BOOK PROJECT came at a very inconvenient time. My elderly mother-in-law unexpectedly became my responsibility because of a health crisis. Then the trauma of placing her in a nursing home was followed by a long-planned month of ministry in Nigeria. It seemed impossible to concentrate on the task of writing and editing.

Then, with little time to prepare, my husband and I moved from a house to an apartment. Our household was in chaos. Everything we needed was out of reach in boxes. Finding the power cord to my typewriter was like a search and destroy mission. My own reference books were buried in storage, so I had to check out the same titles from the Bible school library.

I wrote the chapter on spiritual warfare feeling I was literally "in the trenches." Every imaginable hindrance conspired to deter the work at hand. Meanwhile, family and friends, well aware of the enemy's opposition, covered Quin and me and this project with much prayer.

I really wanted to work on the book (I repeatedly told myself) . . . but at a more convenient time . . . *after* I had everything organized.

Then I thought about Noah. I'm sure he too had many legitimate projects to complete when God gave him the incredible assignment to build an ark.

Noah couldn't fulfill this task at his own convenience or in his spare time. To obey God he had to sweat, get his hands dirty, and give it priority.

The Bible records, "Noah did everything just as God commanded him" (Genesis 6:22). It was important for the sake of his family. The storm was coming.

Just as Noah revised his priorities to build the ark, just as I put aside my personal agenda to meet this deadline, so each of us must make a sacrifice of time and effort to pray for our family and friends. We can't be casual about it. We want them to come into the ark before the storm hits.

I pray that this book will motivate you to pray for your family and friends, and also provide helpful guidelines for doing it.

In this new decade let us be diligent and persistent to fulfill the call to prayer. In the light of eternity, it is probably the most important thing we will do in this life.

—Ruthanne Garlock
January, 1990.

Appendix

Examples of when parents asked Jesus something on behalf of children:

1. Bringing children to him to be blessed: Mark 10:13-16; Matthew 19:13-15; Luke 18:15-17.

2. Royal official asked Jesus to heal his son who was near death: John 4:47-49.

3. Jairus's daughter had died and Jesus came to raise her: Matthew 9:18; Mark 5:22-23.

4. A father sought deliverance for a son with a spirit: Matthew 17:14-16; Luke 9:38-42.

Taking a friend to Jesus:

1. Centurion whose servant was paralyzed asked Jesus to come heal him: Matthew 8:6; Luke 7:1-10.

2. Sick man taken by four friends to Jesus for healing: Mark 2:1-12.

Jesus' Teaching on Prayer:

Matthew	Mark	Luke	John
6:5-18	11:23-26	6:28	14:12-17
7:7-11		10:2	16:23-28
9:37-38		11:1-13	
18:18-20		18:1-14	
21:21-22		21:34-36	

Other Scriptures Pertaining to Prayer in Book of Acts:

1:13-14	4:23-31	9:5-19	14:23
1:24-25	6:4-6	10:1-48	16:13-18
2:42	7:59-60	12:5-17	16:25-34
3:1	8:14-24	13:2-3	28:8

Notes

Chapter Six

1. Theresa Mulligan, "On Really Being A Good Neighbor," *Breakthrough* Newsletter, November/December 1989, Vol. 9, No. 6, pp. 1, 2. (Breakthrough, Inc., Lincoln, VA), Used with permission.
2. Ibid.

Chapter Nine

1. William Gurnall, *The Christian in Complete Armour*, Vol. 1, abridged edition (Banner of Truth Trust: Edinburgh, Scotland and Carlisle, PA, 1986), pp. 140, 141.
2. Paul Billheimer, *Destined for the Throne* (Christian Literature Crusade: Fort Washington, PA, 1975), pp. 17, 18. Used with permission.
3. Ibid., p. 109.
4. Arthur Wallis, *God's Chosen Fast* (Christian Literature Crusade: Fort Washington, PA, Eastbourne, E. Sussex: Kingsway Publications, 1968), pp. 41, 42. Used with permission.
5. Ibid., p. 8.
6. Paul Billheimer, Op., Cit., p. 118.
7. Ibid., p. 67.

Chapter Eleven

1. Jack Hayford, *Prayer Is Invading the Impossible* (New York: Ballantine Books, 1983), pp. 49-51 (© by Logos International, 1977; quoted with permission of the author).
2. Dr. Charles Stanley, *Handle with Prayer* (Wheaton: Victor Books, a division of Scripture Press, 1982) pp. 26, 27.
3. John Dawson, *Taking Our Cities for God* (Lake Mary, FL: Creation House, 1989), pp. 203, 204. Used with permission.
4. Basil Miller, *George Müller—Man of Faith and Miracles* (Minneapolis: Dimension Books, Bethany Fellowship), pp. 145, 146 (© MCMXLI by Zondervan Publishing House).
5. Roger Steer, *George Müller: Delighted in God,* (Wheaton: Harold Shaw Publishers, 1975), p. 310 (© by Roger Steer).

Other Books of Interest
from Servant Publications

The Believer's Guide to Spiritual Warfare
Wising up to Satan's Influence in Your World
Thomas B. White

Learn how to recognize spiritual attack, pray for deliverance, break generational curses, and protect yourself and your family in an age of growing darkness. Tom White introduces believers to the war around them and instructs them in a biblically-based approach to spiritual warfare. *$8.95*

What's Happening to My World?
Standing against the Forces that Threaten Your Children, Your Marriage, Your Neighbors—and Your Sanity
Dee Jepsen

Explore with Dee Jepsen what it means to live out Christian values that give security, not merely for today but for eternity. Discover ways to protect your children and nurture a healthy family. Learn how to let God sovereignly rule your life and use you as a channel for his power in this dark and needy world. *$8.95*

Available at your Christian bookstore or from:
**Servant Publications • Dept. 209 • P.O. Box 7455
Ann Arbor, Michigan 48107**
Please include payment plus $2.75 per book
for postage and handling.
*Send for our FREE catalog of Christian
books, music, and cassettes.*